I0413610

Cory Booker:
Promises Kept &
Promises Broken

1st edition, April 16th, 2017

Edited by Jesse Gordon,
OnTheIssues.org and Ballotpedia.org

Table of Contents

* indicates broken promise

3. Cory Booker on Social Issues 78

4. Cory Booker on National Security Issues 104

5. Cory Booker Political Philosophy 138

* indicates broken promise

Introduction

Do politicians follow through on their campaign promises? Or do they instead show their true colors once elected, having campaigned on whatever issues could get win them the job? This book series answers those questions. In this volume we explore 60 different topics, and compare Cory Booker's campaign promises on each topic with his actions in the U.S. Senate (and sometimes his actions as Newark mayor). The bottom line? We found that Booker followed through on his campaign promises on 44 of those 60 issues – or in other words, that Booker broke his campaign promise on 16 of those 60 issues. That's a "kept promise ratio" of 73% or, in other words, a "broken promise ratio" of 27%. That's better than some politicians, and worse than some others – we think it's pretty typical that elected officials break their promises about ¼ of the time.

Most people will use this book as a reference source – to look up their pet issue to see where Booker stands on that issue, or perhaps reading about a broken promise on a related issue. We try to make that easy by highlighting all the broken promises in the table of contents on pp. 2-3, and in each of our four chapter's issue lists on pp. 10, 42, 78, and 104. The issue lists show a "headline" for each issue as a campaign promise and then a second headline summarizing actions taken in office. Each issue occupies two pages, the left side for Booker's "campaign promise" in context, and the right side for Booker's "Action Taken" in context. We provide additional background when needed on less well-known issues, and a complete analysis of how we drew our conclusion about whether Booker kept his promise or broke it.

In our 5th and final chapter, we synthesize all of Booker's kept promises and broken promises into a "political philosophy" encapsulating his political stances as a campaigner, in comparison with his political stances in office. In summary, Booker campaigned as a moderate liberal, but governs as a libertarian-leaning progressive – we substantiate that claim with a full chapter, using the "VoteMatch quiz" that has been a staple of the OnTheIssues.org website since 1999.

A core concept of this book is transparency: you can trace backwards how we came to our "political philosophy" conclusions, and also trace back to the original sources how we concluded whether Booker kept or broke his promises on each issue. You might disagree with some of our judgment calls – but you can see *HOW* we made those judgment calls, and substitute your judgment for ours to see how that would yield different results. And you can determine whether our VoteMatch quiz gets *YOUR* political philosophy right by taking our do-it-yourself 20-question quiz on pp. 147-50.

What counts as a "broken promise" ?

We don't care *WHAT* politicians say, in this book series, we only care about whether they *DO* what they say and how it compares to their actions. Sometimes Booker made campaign promises that were distinctively conservative – such as his charter schools stance on pp. 100-1 – but as long as he *STAYS* conservative on that issue in his actions in office, we rate that as a "kept promise." In other words, we compare Cory Booker to *HIMSELF*, not to any Democratic standard or progressive standard. (We do, however, compare Booker to *THOSE* standards in our "analysis" comments).

We categorize broken promises into the four categories below. You might dicker about whether one category or another counts as a "broken promise," and politicians might call them "justifications." But our judgment is based on a clear-cut unambiguous definition: If Booker led voters to expect he would behave one way in office, and then he behaved differently, that is a "broken promise," regardless of the precise details about *WHY* he differed on that particular issue. The four categories of "broken promises" are:

1. ***Evolution:*** Did Booker change his opinion over time, as American opinion changed? Or as decisive evidence mounted against his preferred policy? Or as his responsibilities changed from local to national? These are often legitimate reasons for "evolving" on the politician's part – but changing your mind as an elected official means that voters expected a particular policy outcome and got a different policy outcome. For example, Booker's stance evolved on "Broken Windows" crime enforcement because he discovered that it was ineffective. Booker's ***evolution*** include broken promises on these topics:

2. *Legalism:* Does Booker make a legal or technical distinction in his Senate behavior compared to his campaign promises? One that voters might say *TECHNICALLY* is not a broken promise, but which typical voters did not expect? Politicians might call this "nuance" or "subtle policy differences" – but we call them "broken promises." For example, Booker distinguishes between a "carbon tax" and the more general case of a government incentive for green energy – we think that voters would hear the more general case as definitive, and hence scored Booker's legalistic nuance as misleading. Booker's *legalisms* include broken promises on these topics:

3. *Obfuscation*: Did Booker intentionally *muddy the water* with confusing rhetoric, to distract voters? Does he make policy distinctions where normal voters do not? Or make false claims against his opponents to avoid discussing his own stances? Or claim "no comment" when asked, pretending not to have an opinion on key issue? For example, Booker claimed (falsely) that his opponents support school vouchers but never actually disclaimed his own support of vouchers – he intentionally misled voters about others' support of vouchers, and hence about his own stance on vouchers. We avoid the term "*obfuscation*" to avoid muddying the water ourselves; Booker *muddies-the-water* on these topics:

4. *Self-Contradiction:* Did Booker make conflicting promises, so that he *HAD* to break one or the other? Or did his duties require him to "de-prioritize" one goal in favor of another? In either case, voters believed Booker would do one thing, and he did another –

hence they're broken promises. Booker **contradicts** himself on these topics:

Why Cory Booker?

Senator Cory Booker (D-NJ) was first elected to the Senate in October 2013, in a special election to replace Sen. Frank Lautenberg, who died in office earlier that year. Booker was re-elected to a full six-year term in November 2014, and will be up for re-election in 2020.

Prior to his election to the U.S. Senate, Booker was elected as mayor of Newark in 2006 and re-elected in 2010. Booker ran unsuccessfully for mayor in 2002; his 2006 victory was a rematch against the same incumbent. Booker served on the Newark City Council from 1998 to 2002.

Booker hence has six political campaigns from which we can draw campaign promises. And he is in his fourth year in the U.S. Senate, enough time to let his views be known on many topics. When necessary, we also look at his record in office as mayor, especially on issues of local relevance that are not addressed often at the federal level.

Booker's experience – six campaigns over a period of 19 years; four years in legislative office; and seven years in executive office – make him an ideal subject for analysis of campaign promises versus actions taken in office. We also cover less ideal subjects in this book series – as long as they have a couple of campaigns under their belt, and as well as several years of legislative and/or executive experience.

But Booker has a special place too – he is among the frontrunners for the 2020 Democratic presidential nomination. Booker usually identifies himself as a member of the "progressive wing" of the Democratic Party – we explore in detail in this book where Booker is progressive and where he is, instead more liberal, more moderate, or more libertarian (we conclude that he is, indeed, progressive, and we define the term fully in chapter 5). Other progressives in the running for the 2020 Democratic nomination include Senator Elizabeth Warren (D-

MA); Senator Bernie Sanders (I-VT); and Senator Amy Klobuchar (DFL-MN). Other moderates and liberals in the running for 2020 include Senator Tim Kaine (D-VA); Governor John Hickenlooper (D-CO); Secretary Hillary Clinton (D-NY); and Vice President Joe Biden (D-DE). This book series will expand to include them, too, over time.

How does it work?

We attempt to pick representative excerpts from Booker's campaign, and compare them to representative excerpts from his actions in office. Many media sources engage in "selection bias" by picking non-representative excerpts, or presenting just a little snippet out of context – that is biased analysis. We consciously avoid both of those problems by selecting relevant excerpts in their context.

We then encapsulate the relevant aspect in a "headline," which we include with the excerpt and in the summary tables of contents. The "headlines" indicate the part of the excerpt on which we base our decision whether Booker kept his promise or not.

We select excerpts (and headlines) from Cory Booker's page on the website OnTheIssues.org – our archive of Booker's campaign promises as well as his actions taken in office. But we added plenty in order to fill in the blanks, when we had only one side or the other!

We further summarize every topic into one of our 20 questions on our "VoteMatch quiz" in chapter 5 (details of the methodology for VoteMatch can be found there). When Booker has broken a promise, we indicate how his change in policy stance affects his inferred answer to one of the 20 questions, and how it affects his "political philosophy."

Booker's "political philosophy" is calculated from his responses to the 20 questions on VoteMatch, using a two-dimensional analysis instead of the simplistic one-dimensional left-right analysis of the mainstream media. Analyzing Booker's stances on two dimensions – social or economic – allows us to distinguish progressives from liberals, and libertarians from conservatives.

Who wrote this book?

OnTheIssues.org and Ballotpedia.org collaborate in producing the book series "Promises Kept & Promises Broken." The books are used by, and were partly funded by, political organizations interested in the 2018 elections and 2020 elections.

OnTheIssues.org was founded in 1999 to address the gaping hole in political coverage in the mainstream media: political news organizations only report "news." Their definition of news includes the "horse race" of who is ahead in the polls; the "money race" of who is ahead in fundraising; hairstyles and dress and appearance and "optics"; breathless "breaking coverage" of the scandal of the day; and numerous other topics of quickly-passing "news" interest.

OnTheIssues instead covers issues. It's not as exciting or glamorous, but it is what voters should know, in order to cast their votes for candidates in an informed and meaningful way. We applaud news organizations that perform "fact-checking" and which report policy stances and changes in policy stances – but there are far too few of them. OnTheIssues functions as an archive of what politicians have said and done – regardless of whether that's newsworthy or even new at all.

Ballotpedia.org was founded in 2007 as the online encyclopedia of American politics and elections. Ballotpedia's mission is to inform people about politics by providing accurate and objective information – with neutrality ensured by content only from professional editorial staff of over 60 writers and researchers. Ballotpedia's website looks like political sections of Wikipedia, but without the *sturm-und-drang* of Wikipedia's ever-dueling political factions.

Ballotpedia — and its collaboration with OnTheIssues since 2013 — is sponsored by the Lucy Burns Institute, a non-partisan and non-profit organization headquartered in Middleton, Wisconsin. The Lucy Burns Institute is funded entirely by private contributions, and does not receive government funding.

— Jesse Gordon, Editor-in-Chief, jesse@OnTheIssues.org
First edition: April 16th, 2017

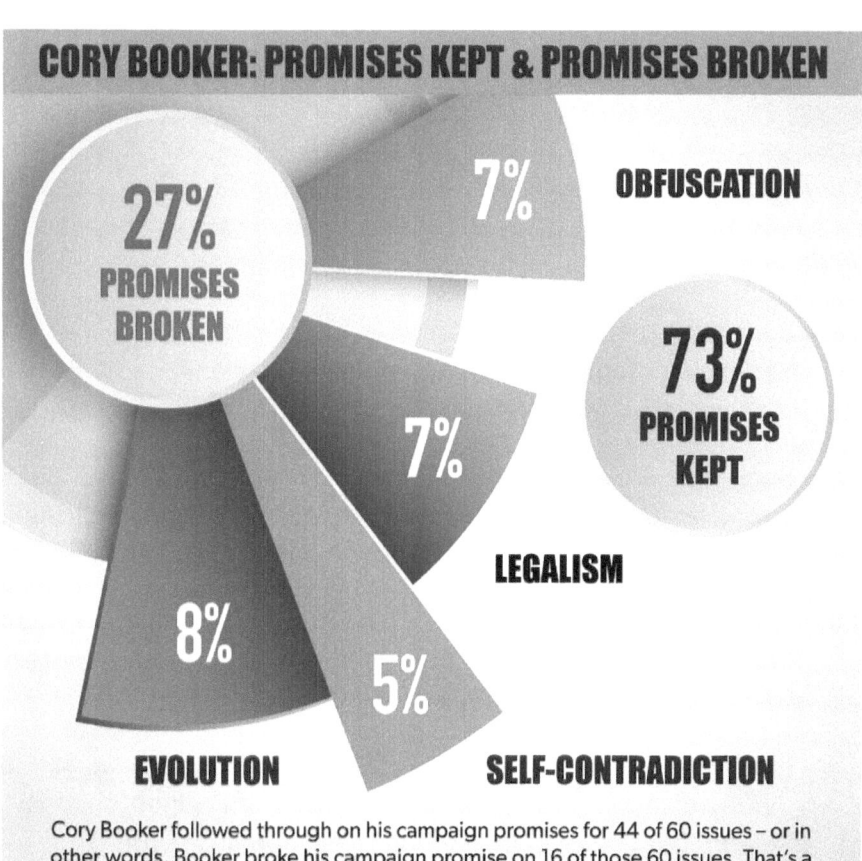

CORY BOOKER: PROMISES KEPT & PROMISES BROKEN

27% PROMISES BROKEN

7% OBFUSCATION

73% PROMISES KEPT

7% LEGALISM

8% EVOLUTION

5% SELF-CONTRADICTION

Cory Booker followed through on his campaign promises for 44 of 60 issues – or in other words, Booker broke his campaign promise on 16 of those 60 issues. That's a "kept promise ratio" of 73% or, in other words, a "broken promise ratio" of 27%.

Chapter One:
Cory Booker on Domestic Issues

* indicates broken promise

* indicates broken promise

Campaign Promises on Gun Proliferation

Insane to carry concealed loaded weapons across state lines

We know we have a gun violence problem in America. The solution is not to get rid of guns. The solution is to have sensible gun laws that keep illegal weapons out of the hands of criminals but also empower communities to make smart choices about how to best protect their neighborhoods, their towns, their cities. Right now moving through our federal legislature is this insane idea that says that people can carry hidden loaded weapons, concealed weapons, all throughout the country regardless of individual state laws. They are basically saying that if in Florida or in Utah, they make a decision to issue a concealed weapon permit, that permit should apply to every other state.

Source: Mayoral website, corybooker.com, Message to Congress, Oct. 18, 2011

KEPT PROMISE: *Booker was elected as mayor promising to take action on gun proliferation, and he did exactly that. Voters expected the same when supporting Booker for Senate – but that promise has proven more problematic (next page).*

ANALYSIS: *Voting for gun control is an easy issue for liberals from urban states like New Jersey. Most urban mayors support voluntary (or involuntary) confiscations, plus numerous restrictions on gun ownership. In rural settings, guns are an inherent part of daily life; liberals from rural states – such as Bernie Sanders from Vermont – often have a more mixed view on gun control.*

If Booker runs for national office, he may "evolve" to a "states' rights" view, that gun control makes sense in New Jersey but not in Vermont, so each state should decide – as hinted at in his Mayor's Coalition excerpt below. That conflicts with his promise above to fight against cross-state gun rights, since that supersedes states' rights. Booker has not yet resolved that conflict in his own policy stances.

Actions Taken on Gun Proliferation

$1,000 reward for tip on illegal weapons

The reason we had four years of double-digit reductions in shootings is that we approached crime as more than just a police issue. We have the first-ever pro bono legal service for ex-offenders. We have one-stop centers for youth coming out of prison; we have a fatherhood program that's gotten a lot of national attention. If you think someone's carrying an illegal gun, all you do is call a tip line. You get four digits, you call back and see if we've made an arrest — we don't need a conviction, we just want to recover the weapon — and then, if we have, you get another four digits that you can use to get $1,000 from a number of local banks. It's just those eight digits, no questions asked.

Source: Andrew Romano interview in Newsweek, Dec. 20, 2010

Coalition "Mayors Against Illegal Guns": keep state laws

As a Coalition of Mayors, we believe that local states should make their own choices and that other people should respect those laws. The laws of Florida when it comes to concealed loaded weapons should not apply to New Jersey. The laws of New Jersey shouldn't necessarily apply to Utah. We cannot have a situation where Congress passes a law and next thing you know, people are showing up in your community with hidden weapons that you, your state legislature, your mayors don't want to have happen. We need each other to respect the laws of our states. And most importantly we need to respect human lives and come together with sensible laws to make sure that our neighborhoods, our towns, our cities, our families can be kept safe and strong and secure.

Source: Mayoral website, corybooker.com, Message to Congress, Oct. 18, 2011

Campaign Promises on Mass Shootings

Common sense gun reform on day one

Passing Common Sense Gun Safety Legislation: It is plainly unacceptable that we don't have background checks for every gun sale in America, as well as bans on high capacity magazines and assault weapons that have no practical sporting use, and countless other reforms that will save lives.

As mayor, I did all I could to fight against gun violence. But now I know that the fight is in Congress. Congress had the chance to get this right in the wake of Newtown. If elected to the Senate, I will start work on common sense gun reform on day one.

Source: CoryBooker.com Senate campaign website, Nov. 3, 2013

Criminals shouldn't have Second Amendment rights

GWEN IFILL: Why do you want to come to Washington in the middle of all this [instead of remaining an effective mayor]?

BOOKER: As mayor, we faced a lot of headwinds because of some of the things that often seem very obvious that Washington isn't doing to help out. So take, for example, gun violence in my city. The majority of guns that we recover don't even come from New Jersey. They come from criminal gun runners who are not law-abiding citizens who should have a Second Amendment right. They come from criminals who can walk into secondary markets and buy weapons. And having commonsense background checks that 90 percent of Americans agree on makes sense, but we're not getting it done.

IFILL: Gun control doesn't seem to be going anywhere, even in the Democratically controlled Senate. Why do you think your presence there would change that?

BOOKER: One senator [can't do it alone]. I've got to work hard & humbly, and find creative ways to join with others to make a difference.

Source: Gwen Ifill interview on PBS "Newshour", Oct. 17, 2013

Actions Taken on Mass Shootings

Failed to pass prohibiting guns to suspected terrorists

Sen. Booker co-sponsored S. Amdt 4720, which died in the U.S. Senate on June 20, 2016. ***Congressional Summary:***

- Authorizes the attorney general to deny the transfer of a firearm if he or she determines that the transferee is a threat to public safety based on a "reasonable" suspicion that the transferee is engaged in terrorism.

- Requires the attorney general to establish a procedure to ensure that if an individual who has been under investigation for terrorism within the previous 5 years attempts to purchase a firearm, the attorney general is promptly notified of the attempt.

Source: Roll call #106 on S.Amdt.4720 to H.R.2578, the Commerce, Justice, Science, & Related Agencies Appropriations Act

BROKEN PROMISE: *Booker attempted and failed as senator to resolve conflicting promises: he promised to fight for gun restrictions, but also promised to collaborate with other senators on guns on "day one" (implying "priority"). That forced a broken promise by* ***self-contradiction.*** *There are not enough anti-gun senators to make that a realistic promise on "day one" – although there are enough anti-gun mayors.*

ANALYSIS: *After the mass shooting at an Orlando nightclub in June 2016, Senate Democrats introduced new gun legislation, including the one above. None passed. Booker pointed out that Congress failed to act "in the wake of Newtown," the 2012 mass shooting, when Booker was mayor – the 2016 Orlando mass shooting, when Booker was senator, was Booker's opportunity to "join with others to make a difference." He failed, although one could argue that it was the Senate that failed.*

Booker's failure was predictable, and accordingly we label this a "Broken Promise." Democrats are aware that they cannot pass gun restrictions nationally – which is why they try only in the wake of mass shootings. Booker misled voters by promising "common sense gun reform on day one" – he knew he would have to await the next gun tragedy. And he also knew that the only SUCCESSFUL approach would be at the state and city level – as he said with his Coalition of Mayors on the previous page – he delivered locally, but could not deliver nationally.

Campaign Promises on Broken Windows Crime Theory

Applied "broken windows theory" in Newark policing

More orthodox strategies have included what's known as the broken windows theory — the idea that attention to basic quality-of-life issues can ultimately help avert serious crimes, as when two policemen stopped a guy drinking a beer on the corner, then discovered he was carrying two guns. When they brought him to the precinct and ran his name through the database, they found out he'd just been released from prison for shooting someone six years earlier on that very corner. "If those cops had driven past the guy, we probably would have had a homicide that night," [Booker's police chief] notes. Overall, [Booker's police policy] is getting results: Murders are down 29 percent since Booker took office, and 2010 saw an almost festive-sounding "murder-free March," the first such month in Newark in more than 40 years. But there have been setbacks.

Source: Oprah Magazine on 2013 N.J. Senate race, Sept. 1, 2010

Long-term believer in "broken windows" theory

Booker remained steadfast in his commitment to reduce crime in the city. He believed that if he could reduce the city's crime rate, not only would the existing residents' quality of life improve, but he would be in a better position to promote the city to businesses and tourists.

Booker has been a long-term believer in the "broken windows" theory, which was made popular by New York City Mayor Rudolph Giuliani. Booker spoke glowingly about this theory to voters during his 2002 campaign, at great political risk. The theory holds that if police officers enforce community standards of decorum (e.g. no loitering, panhandling, littering, squeegee window washing, and the like), criminals will get the message that residents care about their community and will not tolerate crime. This idea led to the belief that police officers can reduce the number of major crimes by enforcing the laws regarding even minor infractions.

Source: The New Black Politician, by Andra Gillespie, p.112, May 7, 2012

Theory of "broken windows" doesn't drive down crime

[The federal DOJ investigated the Newark Police Dept. in 2010]. The report challenged a type of police stop in which I had put great faith — our quality-of-life stop, which stemmed from "broken-windows" theory of policing. The idea is that if you focus on minor infractions that disrupt the quality of life, things that might seem small in the context of more serious crime, you can actually undermine the more serious crime. The theory was widely adopted and is credited by many with playing a role in NYC's success at reducing crime in the 1990s. But they also gave fair warning about how quality-of-life enforcement could undercut the larger goals of a department if there was a lack of legitimacy and equity.

Decades after these practices were documented, judicially upheld and implemented across our nation, the DOJ alleged that our use of stop-and-frisk and quality-of-life summonses were not helping us drive down crime and that these tactics actually undermined residents' quality of life.

Source: United, by Senator Cory Booker, p.154-5, Feb. 16, 2016

BROKEN PROMISE: *The "broken windows" theory is generally considered a Republican theory for crime reduction: take care of small issues like broken windows in inner cities, and the level of respect for the law, and for police, takes hold in the community, leading to reduced crime rates overall. Mayor Booker believed in this theory and applied it to inner-city Newark. Senator Booker "**evolved**" and renounced the theory entirely.*

ANALYSIS: *Booker's turnaround can be attributed to two factors: First, his city's police department was challenged on this issue, and the practice was found counter-productive. Second, the "Black Lives Matter" movement took hold between the time of Booker's time as mayor and his time in the Senate, questioning the effectiveness and the racial bias of many police practices. Both of those factors led Booker to "**evolve**" on this issue. Booker would say that he responded to facts, and to societal change, rather than breaking a campaign promise. But voters who supported Booker because of his beliefs on this issue could feel betrayed.*

Poor & minorities bear the brunt of policing practices

The fact is, poor and minority communities disproportionately bear the brunt of crime. But they also bear the brunt of policing practices that punish their communities — for minor offenses or no offense at all — in ways that wealthier communities simply don't experience. The irony is that communities that are crying out for more police often end up getting a type of policing they aren't seeking and not enough of the police work they need. In a world of budget cuts, we aren't adequately investing in local law enforcement and the strategies that can work, such as community policing, but instead are allowing practices to proliferate that don't reflect our common values.

Source: United, by Senator Cory Booker, p. 155, Feb. 16, 2016

1960s cities had mostly white cops & black majority

Overt racism pervaded Newark in the 1960s. Though blacks and Latinos accounted for the majority of the population, they had almost no meaningful political representation. What's more, mostly white officers policed predominantly black sections of the city, like the Central Ward. There were widespread reports of police brutality, and tensions built up around the all-too-common experiences of black youth who were stopped and harassed by the police.

Source: United, by Senator Cory Booker, p.44 & 55, Feb. 16, 2016

BACKGROUND: The 'Black Lives Matter' movement seeks to get police to stop treating African Americans differently than white suspects. The movement comes to the fore whenever a video emerges from a police shooting of black suspects, as has occurred regularly over the past few years. Saying 'Black Lives Matter' blames the police for institutionalized racism, and demands corrective action by changing how police behave. The counter-movement uses the term 'Blue Lives Matter,' implying support of police in a dangerous job. Booker's language echoes the language of the 'Black Lives Matter' movement, while avoiding using the politicized term itself, because he prefers to build coalitions among all parties.

Actions Taken on Black Lives Matter

Rated 9% by NAPO, indicating a police-the-police stance

Ratings by the National Association of Police Organizations indicate support or opposition to issues of importance to police and crime. The organization's self-description:

"The National Association of Police Organizations (NAPO) is a coalition of police units and associations from across the United States. NAPO was organized for the purpose of advancing the interests of America's law enforcement officers through legislative advocacy, political action, and education. Increasingly, the rights and interests of law enforcement officers have been the subject of legislative, executive, and judicial action in the nation's capital. NAPO works to influence the course of national affairs where law enforcement interests are concerned. The following list includes examples of NAPO's accomplishments:

- Enactment of the Fair Sentencing Act

- Enactment of the National AMBER Alert Act

- Enactment of the Violent Crime Control and Law Enforcement Act

- Enactment of the Adam Walsh Child Protection and Safety Act

- Enactment of the Law Enforcement Officers' Safety Act (Right to Carry Legislation)

Source: NAPO ratings on Congress and politicians on Dec. 31, 2014

KEPT PROMISE: *Booker is an African American urban mayor from a liberal state – whom voters expected to favor Black Lives Matter – and he has delivered on that expectation.*

ANALYSIS: *Mayor Booker attempted rhetorically to maintain good relations with his local police department, but his low rating by a national police organization indicates that most police didn't buy his rhetoric. Most of the legislative acts scored in NAPO's list above would be opposed by the majority of Black Lives Matter advocates and supported by the majority of Blue Lives Matter advocates.*

Campaign Promises on First Responders

Increase the number of police in all neighborhoods

Cory Booker's work as councilman from Newark's Central Ward earned him praise from Newark residents and the New York Times:

- *Local Nuisance Codes:* Organized pro-bono attorneys to fight against drug dealing in local communities through the enforcement of codes.

- *Hunger Strike:* Organized a 10-day Camp Out where the Councilman slept out and went on a hunger strike against drugs and crime in Garden Spires.

- *Police Presence:* (1/19/2000) Fought on the City Council to increase the number of police in all neighborhoods.

- *Additional Security:* Pushed legislation mandating that private buildings provide more security for local residents.

Source: CoryBooker.com Mayoral campaign website, Feb. 7, 2002

Actions Taken on First Responders

Cut first responders due to economic downturn

As an executive serving during the deepest economic downturn this nation has endured in generations, I did all I could to protect the ranks of my fire and police departments, and funding for emergency medical services.

But it wasn't enough. Like most localities in New Jersey, and like so many across the country, we watched our ranks dwindle even as we searched for new revenue and cut everywhere else first.

Source: CoryBooker.com Senate campaign website, Nov. 3, 2013

BROKEN PROMISE: *Booker COULD have said this decision was "evolution" – that he came to realize that a cop on every corner would be harmful to minority residents, in the vein of Black Lives Matter. We suspect this more accurately reflects his personal opinion, but he has not expressed that publicly. We would have scored that as a "Broken Promise by evolution." But he didn't say that, so instead it's a "Broken Promise by de-prioritization," a form of* **self-contradiction** *due to conflicting promises.*

ANALYSIS: *If Booker truly wanted to increase the number of police, he could have arranged his city budget to do so. Funding for more police was about priorities – as is always the case with funding priorities for elected officials. As City Councilor, Booker demanded that the mayor shift priorities to Booker's preferences of more police. But then as mayor himself, he chose other priorities. Booker could defend himself by claiming that circumstances trumped his ability to fulfill his promise – but we think a priority choice in politics is always a choice.*

Campaign Promises on Prison Reform

Incarceration isn't working; focus on recidivism

Our criminal justice system is broken. New Jersey's prison population increased by 328% between 1980 and 2011, burdening taxpayers with billions of dollars in direct and indirect costs, and destabilizing countless families and communities. And that incarceration isn't working: 55% of those who go to state prison are rearrested within three years. In Newark, we didn't wait for the state or federal government to get their act together:

- We launched ex-offender reentry programs that drove down recidivism rates;

- We created a youth court, community court, and veterans court — the community court and veterans court are the first of their kind in the state, designed to connect low level offenders with specialized resources to reduce recidivism and better protect our neighborhoods.

- We expanded mentoring programs, recreation spaces, and youth employment opportunities to engage our kids in constructive activities that lead to productive pathways, not prison.

Source: CoryBooker.com Senate campaign website, Nov. 3, 2013

Prison construction draws funds from other priorities

- The federal incarceration rate has increased 800% and state incarceration rates have increased 500% since 1980.

- Our nation is now the undisputed incarceration capital of the world. America has roughly 5% of the globe's population but about 25% of the imprisoned people on the planet.

- Roughly 1/3 of all adult Americans have an arrest record.

Most Americans don't know the extent of our incarceration explosion, and hearing about it sparks feeling of disbelief. In the years between 1990 and 2005, a new prison opened EVERY TEN DAYS. The astonishing rate of construction draws precious public resources away from other priorities.

Source: Underlined, by Senator Cory Booker, 165-6, Feb. 16, 2016

Actions Taken on Prison Reform

Decrease prison population
by reducing mandatory minimums

I reintroduced the Smarter Sentencing Act of 2015, bipartisan legislation that would enact meaningful sentencing reforms that would make our federal sentencing policy fairer, smarter, and more cost-effective. It would reduce harsh mandatory minimums for nonviolent drug offenders, which is the single largest factor in the growth of the federal prison population. If we want our prison population to decrease, we must reduce mandatory minimums.

The bill would expand the federal "safety valve," which returns discretion in sentencing for nonviolent drug offenses back to federal judges. It would allow persons convicted under the pre-2010 crack cocaine laws to receive reduced sentences, a change needed to make crack cocaine penalties more in line with powder cocaine penalties. Crack and powder cocaine are pharmacologically the same. The Smarter Sentencing Act would reduce these sentences and save our country $229 million over the next 10 years.

Source: Brennan Center for Justice essays, p. 10-1, April 28, 2015

KEPT PROMISE: *Booker took the progressive "prison reform" stance as mayor, as a Senate candidate, and as senator: focusing on the "prison industry" as a self-serving business, rather than as a means of implementing justice.*

ANALYSIS: *The U.S. Senate has only limited power in prison reform, because much prison policy is handled at the state level. Hence Booker focuses above on federal sentencing reform on federal drug issues. Most voters would interpret that, correctly, as also desiring state sentencing reform on state crime issues, as Booker discussed as a candidate.*

Campaign Promises on Marijuana Legalization

Supports medical marijuana and reducing drug arrests

Newark Mayor Cory Booker took to Reddit Sunday to criticize the war on drugs, saying it was ineffective and "represents big overgrown government at its worst."

The Democrat wrote during the Reddit "ask me anything" chat: "The so called War on Drugs has not succeeded in making significant reductions in drug use, drug arrests or violence. We are pouring huge amounts of our public resources into this current effort that are bleeding our public treasury and unnecessarily undermining human potential."

Booker then called drug arrests a "game": "My police in Newark are involved in an almost ridiculous game of arresting the same people over and over again and when you talk to these men they have little belief that there is help or hope for them to break out of this cycle," he wrote.

Booker has said he supports medical marijuana, and outlined programs he has implemented to lower drug arrests: reentry, court reform, jobs, treatment and legal aid.

Source: "Cory Booker Slams Drug War," by Ethan Klapper, Huffington Post, July 16, 2012

Community courts for minor crimes like drug possession

Community courts zero in on low-level crime — offenses like vandalism, shoplifting, minor drug possession — and combine punishment and help. In the community court, instead of fines many people can't pay or short jail terms that do them no good, quality-of-life offenders will be sentenced to visible community service throughout the City and referred to drug treatment, job training, adult education, counseling and other services. Research suggests that this problem-solving approach to justice works: community courts in other cities have helped reduce crime while improving public trust and involvement in the justice system. I am so proud of the collaborative effort...

Source: State of the City Address at Newark Symphony Hall, Feb. 9, 2009

Actions Taken on Marijuana Legalization

Rated B+ by NORML, indicating a pro-legalization stance

OnTheIssues.org interprets the 2016 NORML scores for all Members of Congress as follows:

- C-/D/F: "hard-on-drugs" stance (approx. 243 members)
- C: mixed record on drug reform (approx. 45 members)
- A/B: pro-drug-reform stance (approx. 293 members)

About NORML (from their website, www.norml.org): National Organization for the Reform of Marijuana Law's mission is to move public opinion sufficiently to achieve the repeal of marijuana prohibition so that the responsible use of cannabis by adults is no longer subject to penalty.

NORML supports the removal of all criminal penalties for the private possession & responsible use of marijuana by adults, including the cultivation for personal use, and the casual nonprofit transfers of small amounts. This model is called "decriminalization." NORML additionally supports the development of a legally controlled market for marijuana, where consumers could purchase it from a safe, legal and regulated source. This model is referred to as "legalization."

NORML strongly supports the right of patients to use marijuana as a medicine when their physician recommends it to relieve pain and suffering.

Source: NORML congressional ratings, Nov. 8, 2016

KEPT PROMISE: *Booker has consistently supported marijuana decriminalization, both in his campaigns and in his voting record and mayoral record.*

ANALYSIS: *Booker claims as his rationale that marijuana enforcement is ineffective – grouping his drug policy with his crime policy, that enforcing marijuana laws is a quality-of-life issue like the "Broken Windows" theory. Under that framework, Booker was inconsistent as mayor by supporting "Broken Windows" enforcement while opposing marijuana enforcement. His current stance has now become consistent between these two issues.*

Campaign Promises on War on Drugs

The drug war is an abject failure

As homicides surge in the city he governed for seven years, Booker said he's looking at several programs to overhaul the US criminal justice system and end the war on drugs, which he said fuels much of the violence.

"I can say as a mayor who has been fighting on the front lines for years, the drug war is an abject failure," Booker said. "It's consumed egregious amounts of taxpayers' dollars. It hasn't achieved the public-safety aims of our streets, it's consumed human potential, it is a massive government overreach."

He said the real answer to fighting crime is addressing poverty and poor education. "All of these things are things we should be working collaboratively on," Booker said.

Source: Newark Star-Ledger on New Jersey Senate race, Jan. 1, 2014

Give addicts treatment instead of long sentences

Some of the most important work we need to do to reduce crime has nothing to do with police. I am proud more people are realizing the importance of giving addicts treatment instead of longer sentences behind bars. I am proud that there is a growing awareness of America's unmet mental health needs.

We are also coming to realize how essential it is to dismantle the school-to-prison pipeline — the ridiculous policies that have criminalized kids instead of nurturing them, helping them, & healing them. There is a growing body of research that shows we can lower crime rates by better dealing with childhood trauma and investing in policies such as Nurse-Family Partnerships, where at-risk mothers get home nurse visits that are proven to reduce the cost to taxpayers of everything from kids' emergency room visits to teens' encounters with the police.

Source: United, by Senator Cory Booker, p.157-8, Feb. 16, 2016

Actions Taken on War on Drugs

Keep ObamaCare's prevention, treatment, and recovery services

Repealing the Affordable Care Act (ACA) with no clear plan for replacement will substantially worsen the opioid epidemic. Last year, Congress took important steps to address this national public health crisis, enacting two laws to address the opioid epidemic and reform the way our health system treats mental health and substance use disorders.

The Comprehensive Addiction and Recovery Act improved access to substance use disorder prevention, treatment, and recovery services. It promoted the use of best practices when prescribing opioid pain-killers, strengthening state prescription drug monitoring programs, and expanding access to the life-saving drug naloxone.

The 21st Century Cures Act included critical mental health and substance use disorder reforms, strengthening enforcement of mental health parity laws, and promoting an expanded mental health workforce. Most importantly, the Act dedicated $1 billion in new grant funding to help states provide prevention, treatment, and recovery services.

These bipartisan advances will be fundamentally undermined by repeal of the Affordable Care Act. Repealing the mental health and substance use disorder coverage provisions of the ACA would withdraw at least $5.5 billion annually from the treatment of low income people with mental and substance use disorders — more than ten times greater than the funding increase included in the 21st Century Cures Act.

Source: Letter to Pres. Donald Trump from 20 senators, Feb. 6, 2017

KEPT PROMISE: *Booker objects to the War on Drugs because its criminal enforcement has been ineffective, and has long advocated for social investment to replace that criminal enforcement.*

ANALYSIS: *As senator, Booker collaborates to refocus the Drug War on treatment rather than enforcement – in other words, converting drugs to a health issue from a criminal issue.*

Drug war isn't waged in privileged communities

I knew, from living in the relatively privileged communities I grew up in, that the drug war wasn't waged in those places like it was in Newark. I was coming from college campuses and towns where marijuana, ecstasy, cocaine, and other drugs were widespread and often used openly, with little fear of the police.

The war on drugs has turned out to be a war on *PEOPLE* — and far too often a war on people of color and the poor. Marijuana use, for example, is roughly equal among blacks and whites, yet blacks are 3.7 times more likely to be arrested for possession than whites.

Further, there is no difference between blacks and whites in dealing drugs. In fact, some studies show that whites are more likely than blacks to sell drugs, even though blacks are far more likely to be arrested for it.

Source: United, by Senator Cory Booker, p.181, Feb. 16, 2016

Minorities imprisoned for drugs at 6 times whites

More than 60 percent of the prison population is comprised of racial and ethnic minorities. This is driven by wide disparities in arrests and incarceration. Even though blacks and Latinos engage in drug offenses at a rate no different than whites, blacks are incarcerated at a rate six times greater than whites, and Latinos are incarcerated at nearly twice the rate of whites for the same offenses. The incarceration rate of Native Americans is 38 percent higher than the national rate. Latinos account for 17 percent of the U.S. population, but 22 percent of the U.S. incarcerated population. And, blacks make up only 13 percent of the total U.S. population, but 37 percent of the U.S. prison population. Today, we have more black men in prison or under state or federal supervision than were enslaved in 1850.

Source: Brennan Center for Justice essays, p. 9, April 28, 2015

Actions Taken on Opioid Crisis

Criminalize imports of opioid precursors

We write to request the European Commission's assistance in addressing a significant aspect of the opioid epidemic that is killing Americans at alarming rates. The United Nations International Narcotics Control Board is considering designating NPP and ANPP, which are precursor chemicals of the synthetic opioid fentanyl, as Table I substances under the 1988 UN Convention against Illicit Traffic in Narcotic Drugs and Psychotropic Substances.

Currently, the unregulated purchase of NPP and ANPP is perfectly consistent with current international law because these chemicals are not currently controlled under international drug treaties. NPP and ANPP are already controlled in the U.S. under the Controlled Substances Act, which imposes licensing and approved use requirements. However, without collective international action it will be difficult to control international manufacture, distribution and sales of NPP and ANPP, and as a result will frustrate efforts to curb manufacturing and trafficking of illicit fentanyl.

We believe that the 1988 Convention could be a critical tool in regulating the sale and export of NPP and ANPP. We would greatly appreciate support from the European Commission for the U.S. request to designate NPP and ANPP as Table I substances.

*Source: Letter to President of the European Commission
from 17 senators, Feb. 17, 2017*

BROKEN PROMISE: *Booker adopts on the opposite page a strongly progressive stance on crime and drugs – that drug enforcement is racially biased. He "**evolved**" and signed on to the War on Opioids.*

ANALYSIS: *Some progressives and minority voters would consider the "opioid epidemic" just the latest application of biased enforcement, and would expect Booker to apply his racial-bias philosophy to a general rejection of drug enforcement. Booker would differentiate opioids as more dangerous than marijuana — which critics would say follows in the scare-tactic footsteps of Demon Rum and Reefer Madness. Booker's proposed border interdiction above is a standard proposal of Drug Warriors – just involving international institutions as a novel feature.*

Campaign Promises on Voter Suppression

Threat to voting rights in America remains very real

As we've seen on several recent occasions, most notably in the Texas redistricting plan that federal courts last year described as intentionally discriminatory, the threat to voting rights in America remains very real. The Voting Rights Act has been instrumental in the fight against violations of one of our most precious constitutional rights, and Congress must now act decisively in the wake of the Supreme Court's damaging decision and put in place updated, robust protections that once again give teeth to this vital law.

Source: CoryBooker.com Senate campaign website, Nov. 3, 2013

BACKGROUND: *The voter registration issue has been brewing since the 2000 presidential race was determined by the purge of Florida's voting rolls. Republicans favor "Voter Identification" requirements, on the grounds of ensuring the integrity of the vote. Democrats respond that individual voter fraud is extremely rare and has not ever affected an election outcome. The partisan reason for these stances is that voter identification discourages voting by youth, minorities, and the elderly, all of whom disproportionately favor Democrats. In 2013 and 2014, courts struck down voter ID requirements in Pennsylvania, Wisconsin and Arkansas, but other requirements persist in 31 other states.*

KEPT PROMISE: *Booker believes, like most progressives, that restrictions on voting are racially motivated. His vote is assured on any major aspect of voting reform.*

ANALYSIS: *This is an active fight in the courts and in Congress, and Booker has taken an active role in the fight. This is one of the few issues where the Green Party and the Libertarian Party simultaneously agree with the Democratic Party – because voting restrictions hurt third parties and all establishment outsiders.*

Actions Taken on Voter Suppression

Automatic voter registration for all citizens

Booker co-sponsored H.R.12 & S.1088, the Voter Empowerment Act; Congressional Summary:

- Require each state to make available official public websites for online voter registration.

- Authorizes automated voter registration and establishes same day registration, and voter registration of individuals under 18 years of age.

- Declares that the right to vote shall not be denied because that individual has been convicted of a criminal offense.

Supporters reasons for voting YEA: (Brennan Center): Too many Americans go to vote on Election Day only to find their names are not on the voter rolls — often, wrongly deleted. The US is on the verge of a new paradigm for registering voters: automatic, permanent registration of eligible voters, which adds up to 50 million eligible voters to the rolls.

Opponents reasons for voting NAY: (Gov. Christie's veto message on the "Democracy Act", Nov. 2015): Christie called a provision establishing automatic voter registration that requires a New Jersey citizen an to opt out is a "government-knows-best, backwards approach that would inconvenience citizens and waste government resources for no justifiable reason." Automatic voter registration would have added 1.6 million people to the state's voter rolls.

(PopVox.org blogger from TN-8): I have voted in every election federal, state or local that I chose to. If people want to vote there is nothing but laziness preventing them from doing so today! Regarding photo ID's you have one to drive, buy alcohol, and go to the doctor.

(PopVox.org blogger from AL-2): This bill is so general that anyone that is alive, has lived, or will live in this century will be able to vote as well as non-Americans, pets, people without voting rights, and some people multiple times.

Source: Voter Empowerment Act on March 19, 2015

Campaign Promises on Digital Divide

Invest in Next-Gen air traffic; broadband, and smart grid

Increase funding for Next Gen Satellite-based airplane traffic control system: A safe and efficient air travel system, capable of transporting people and cargo across the country and all over the world, is central to our economy. But the U.S. air traffic control system — a ground-based, radar system developed in the 1950s — has not been upgraded in decades. With Next-Gen GPS-based technology, businesses can count on a faster and more reliable air transport system, with shorter flights, and fewer delays and cancellations.

Bring broadband to underserved urban and rural communities: Nearly 19 million Americans are without broadband internet access. This is unacceptable in today's interconnected society. Broadband is vital to small businesses, students who we will rely upon to fill tomorrow's jobs, consumers who want to access the best products at the lowest prices, and citizens who want to more robustly engage in our democracy. The internet unlocks worlds of opportunity, and no one should be deprived of the key.

Create a national smart grid: Upgrading our electric grid to allow businesses, homes, and other end users to send energy use data back to utilities increases resiliency and stability, and can empower businesses and consumers to use energy more efficiently. Smart grid spending also helps our economy — generating a more than two-to-one return on investment.

Source: CoryBooker.com Senate campaign website, July 1, 2014

BACKGROUND: *The 'Digital Divide' refers to good Internet access among middle- and upper-income people, with poorer access, if any, among lower-income people, especially in schools. Generally, discussing the 'Digital Divide' means favoring subsidies for better Internet access in urban schools.*

KEPT PROMISE: *Booker promised to support technological infrastructure projects, and has followed through.*

Actions Taken on Digital Divide

Support Lifeline program for low-income broadband

We write to express how deeply troubled we are that one of your first actions as Chairman of the Federal Communications Commission has been to undermine the Lifeline program and make it more difficult for low-income people to access affordable broadband. Lifeline is a critical tool for closing the digital divide — a problem you pledged to prioritize in your first speech to FCC staff as Chairman. Accordingly, we urge you to reverse your decision to abruptly revoke the recognition of nine companies as Lifeline broadband providers (LBP) just weeks after they were approved. This action does nothing but create a chilling effect on potential provider participation, and unfairly punish low-income consumers.

Established during the Reagan Administration, the Lifeline program has helped millions of low-income Americans afford basic phone service. Last year, the FCC modernized the Lifeline program, rightfully refocusing its support on broadband, which helps end the cruel "homework gap" for the five million out of the 28 million households in this country with school-aged children who lack access to broadband.

By statute, the FCC has an obligation to ensure "consumers in all regions of the country, including low-income consumers" have access to "advanced telecommunications services." Expanding broadband adoption by low-income families provides a foundation for long-term economic development. We call on you to reconsider your decision.

Source: Letter to FCC chairman from 15 senators, Feb. 10, 2017

ANALYSIS: Infrastructure, in general, is a core issue for progressives because much infrastructure entails societal spending with poorer people as the primary beneficiaries. Other political groups might support infrastructure for defense, or for local development, but not for income redistribution. That's the progressive rationale for every infrastructure improvement from pubic roads and public libraries in the past to free Internet access in the present.

Campaign Promises on Infrastructure

Fix crumbling infrastructure with
National Infrastructure Bank

The 2012 federal transportation bill notes, "the condition and capacity of the highway system has failed to keep up with the growth in freight movement and is hampering the ability of businesses to efficiently transport goods due to congestion."

American rail infrastructure, once considered the best in the world, now ranks eighteenth, plagued by congested choke points and crossings that force trains to travel at inefficient low speeds.

This has real economic consequences: a weak national infrastructure not only raises production costs and reduces productivity for American businesses, but also discourages foreign investment and development. We can create jobs and strengthen our infrastructure for decades to come by creating a national infrastructure bank that leverages public funding to increase private investment in American roads, bridges, airports, marine ports and other assets.

Source: CoryBooker.com Senate campaign website, July 1, 2014

Businesses realize a return on infrastructure investment

We all know — it's common sense — that for an economy built to last we must invest in what will fuel us for generations to come. This is our history — from the Transcontinental Railroad to the Hoover Dam, to the dredging of our ports and building of our most historic bridges — our American ancestors prioritized growth and investment in our nation's infrastructure.

And today our businesses, industries, entrepreneurs and economy realize a return on those investments. Let us not fall prey to rhetoric that seeks to gut investment and starve our nation of critical, common-sense building for our future. And investment must include the real engine of job growth in America: the American small business.

Source: Democratic National Convention speech, Sept. 4, 2012

Actions Taken on Infrastructure

We can't afford to ignore aging infrastructure anymore

Officials highlighted the planned extension of the Hudson-Bergen Light Rail (HBLR) as a catalyst for job creation, economic growth and improved quality of life.

"Even in a divided Washington, infrastructure investment shouldn't be a partisan issue," said Sen. Booker. "I believe we can unite Republicans and Democrats around this issue and get something done. We can't afford to ignore the aging infrastructure anymore. Failing to make the necessary developments in infrastructure is not only crippling our competitiveness in a global economy, it's crippling hard-working New Jerseyans' opportunities to excel here at home. I will continue to work for long-term investment in infrastructure that creates jobs, stimulates economic growth, and improves the quality of our public transportation."

The federal lawmakers also urged their colleagues in Washington to pass a long-term fix to fully fund the Highway Trust Fund (HTF), which will go bankrupt in this summer.

Source: Press Release from NJ congressional delegation, March 13, 2015

BACKGROUND: *In 2008, President Obama backed proposed legislation for a National Infrastructure Reinvestment Bank. Obama suggested that the Bank would borrow $60 billion to invest in infrastructure over 10 years, while leveraging "up to $500 billion" of private investment. No legislation resulted. President Trump has repeated the same call in 2017.*

KEPT PROMISE: *Booker promised to push infrastructure investment, and he has taken collaborative action in the Senate to attempt to do so. Whether he is successful is entirely up to the Republican-controlled Congress and President Trump.*

ANALYSIS: *Booker's rationale is economic: that infrastructure is an investment that will produce future returns on that investment. President Trump agrees with that rationale, but presidents and Congress have a long history of promising infrastructure investment and never delivering, because infrastructure projects get accused of being "pork barrel" political spending like 2011's "Bridge to Nowhere."*

Campaign Promises on Environmental Protection

Sustainability programs: green space and green jobs

As mayor, I quickly worked to implement sustainability programs that created green jobs, slowed the growth of our carbon footprint, and saved millions of dollars by driving down energy costs.

In 2008, I created Newark's first Office of Sustainability and organized a "Green Future Summit" that brought additional structure to our efforts. In 2013, we released Newark's first ever Sustainability Action Plan, which provides a comprehensive roadmap for making Newark a greener, healthier and more vibrant city. More importantly, these programs have delivered concrete results that will continue to benefit Newarkers long after I leave office. We:

- Raised funds for and executed the largest parks and green-space expansion in Newark in over a century;

- Created a program that trained Newark youth in home weatherization and then placed them in jobs that paid a living wage to do the work in our neighborhoods;

- Secured $1.5 million for a major campaign to expand Newark's tree canopy to reduce the urban heat island effect;

- Pushed successfully for an agreement among state, Port Authority, and private sector leaders to install a new "baghouse filter" on the Covanta Energy facility that will reduce emissions of particulate matter by almost 200 tons per year;

- Partnered to begin clean up of the Passaic River, one of the nation's most serious Superfund sites;

- Created acres of urban farms that now provide fresh produce to underserved neighborhoods.

Source: CoryBooker.com Senate campaign website, Nov. 3, 2013

KEPT PROMISE: *Booker pushes for green space; sustainable development; brownfield cleanup; local agriculture; and other progressive environmental issues – as promised.*

Actions Taken on Environmental Protection

Neighborhood development instead of new sports arena

Booker was highly critical of [mayoral opponent Sharpe] James's focus on big projects. The biggest plan was to build a sports arena in downtown Newark. James made the arena the centerpiece of his 2002 mayoral campaign. Cory Booker was an ardent critic of the arena and of most of James's development projects in 2002. He argued that James focused on downtown development at the expense of neighborhood development. He also thought that the arena project was wasteful.

When Booker was elected mayor in 2006, he tried to enjoin the ground-breaking for the arena. His request was denied, so he was stuck with having to make the best of what he perceived to be a bad situation. Booker's economic development office worked to try to make the arena as much of an economic boon as possible.

Source: The New Black Politician, by A. Gillespie, p.130-1, May 7, 2012

GreenSpaces: public-private partnership for city parks

Citizen activists [work with] businesspeople, social entrepreneurs, and government officials [to break] through bureaucratic rules to improve services while cutting costs and promoting individual freedom.

I'm inspired by stories [about public-private collaborations] because through similar alliances we're transforming life for the people of Newark. Our public-private partnership, GreenSpaces, has brought public parks within reach of thousands of our citizens for the first time in decades.

Source: Foreword to "Citizen You," by Jonathan Tisch, p.x, April 26, 2010

***ANALYSIS:** Booker got elected mayor on this issue of urban development: his predecessor in office, Mayor James Sharpe, preferred business-oriented development, while Booker preferred neighborhood-oriented development.*

Campaign Promises on Animal Rights

Vegetarian because of environmental impact of eating meat

Booker tears into a takeout container of scrambled egg whites with peppers and onions. As Booker describes it in his soothing, storyteller's tenor, "I decided to take to heart Socrates' admonishment about the unexamined life" — the one that says such a life isn't worth living. "And I started reading everything I could. And the more I read, from the environmental impact of eating meat to the health issues to Gandhi, the more I realized that eating the extreme amounts that I really enjoyed was not resonant with my spirit, with my values. So I tried to go cold turkey, and my body just took off — I felt so good. I'm not one of those judgmental vegetarians who says everybody should do this, but for me it works, and it works very well." In a city not known for its salad bars, Booker is an anomaly.

Source: Oprah Magazine article on N.J. Senate race, Sept. 1, 2010

Vegetarian since 1992; vegan since 2014

I had been a vegetarian since 1992 — a lifestyle choice that had started as an experiment. I realized that there was a lot about food I could never fully pin down. After poring over data on health, the environment, and how industrial agriculture treated animals, I thought I should try to go without meat. Did I need it? Was I the master of my desires, or had my desires mastered me? I decided to try being a vegetarian.

Within a couple of months I was astounded by the results. Active as I was, when I went vegetarian my body felt supercharged. I felt energy like I hadn't ever had before. My sleep improved, my recovery after workouts improved, and I felt lighter, stronger and more capable. I never looked back. 22 years later, after more reading, study and self-examination, I decided to try another experiment for the same reasons: from the day after Election Day 2014 until the end of that year, I would try being a vegan. It, too, would become an experiment that would stick.

Source: United, by Senator Cory Booker, p.124-5, Feb. 16, 2016

Actions Taken on Animal Rights

Rated 100% on all animal welfare ratings

Animals and Wildlife organizational ratings:

- 2015-2016 Animal Welfare Institute - Positions 100%

- 2013-2014 Animal Welfare Institute - Positions 100%

- 2015 American Veterinary Medical Association - Positions on Professional Advocacy 100%

- 2014 American Veterinary Medical Association - Positions on Professional Advocacy 100%

- 2015 Food Policy Action - Positions 100%

- 2013-2014 Food Policy Action - Positions 100%

- 2015 Defenders of Wildlife Action Fund - Positions 100%

- 2015 Humane Society Legislative Fund - Positions 100%

Source: Vote-Smart Animals and Wildlife group ratings, Dec. 31, 2016

KEPT PROMISE: *Booker's voters expected his personal veganism to translate to pro-animal policy, and Booker has delivered. Vegetarianism can be a religious obligation, but otherwise, it is usually a political statement. In Booker's case, it has translated into his political philosophy.*

ANALYSIS: *Animal rights is a growing issue in the environmental movement, underlying issues ranging from vegetarianism to closure of dog tracks. As a vegan, Senator Booker is likely to be cited as the "poster boy" for this movement. The core concept is to apply some rights to animals that apply to humans, at some cutoff level of animal intelligence. Most people agree on ending whale hunting, for example, because whales are intelligent; a majority of people agree that animal abuse should be prosecuted; some people apply those rules to all animals and would ban hunting or eating meat. The counterpoint considers the entire animal rights movement to be "political correctness."*

Campaign Promises on Environment vs. Economy

Dumping pollutants into rivers externalizes costs

One American chemical company, Diamond Alkali, started producing Agent Orange in a factory along the Passaic River in Newark — and reportedly dumped "bad" batches of Agent Orange directly into the river. At the same time, the chemicals at the factory site leached into the earth below the factory. Installing catch basins and properly disposing of the chemicals would have added hundreds of thousands of dollars to the business costs; pouring them into the river was the cheaper route for the company — even if far more expensive for the commons.

In 1983 the EPA confirmed what was already know — that the extreme levels of contaminants at the Diamond Alkali plant and in the lower Passaic River posed a grave threat to human life. The EPA added the site to its National Priorities List of Superfund sites around the country, making it eligible for taxpayer-funded cleanup.

This was my environmental awakening [about externalizing pollution costs].

The destruction of the Passaic River is an example of the perversion of the free market. In theory, goods & services are to be priced according to the actual costs of production with an addition of incremental cost for profit. What actually happened in Newark and communities around the country — and continues to happen today — is that key costs of production were shifted onto society while the profits were kept by the enterprise. With their costs externalized, the enterprise's profits increase. In the case of the Passaic River, and in the cases of so many other national treasures, these externalized costs are paid for over and over again by one generation after another.

Source: United, by Senator Cory Booker, p.197, Feb. 16, 2016

Actions Taken on Environment vs. Economy

Trees reduce erosion & increase property values

In our efforts to green our city, we ended up having many discussions about trees. Before these conversations, trees to me were often sources of constituent complaints — fallen branches that needed to be cleared, dead trees that needed to be removed, roots that were pushing up sidewalks. But Newark's activists and leaders educated me on the benefits they provide, and soon we set out to find every way possible to plant more of them. Trees cool a city, provide oxygen, and help clean and filter the air of particulate matter, helping to combat respiratory problems. Trees help reduce storm water runoff, reducing erosion and the pollution that is carried into waterways. They even increase property values, adding beauty and character to a block.

Source: United, by Senator Cory Booker, p.203-4, Feb. 16, 2016

BACKGROUND: *"Externalizing costs" means, for example, that a company which produces a pollutant does not pay for cleanup of that pollutant after production; that cleanup cost is "externalized" to society. A key concept of environmental economics is to "internalize" externalities, which is encapsulated as the "Polluter Pays Principle." Libertarians support lawsuits to enforce that the polluter pays; progressives prefer to build in the cleanup cost earlier in the production process. In both cases, "internalizing" pollution cleanup means the product price reflects both the production cost and the cleanup cost.*

KEPT PROMISE: *Booker promised economically-sound environmental enhancements, and then delivered services that he justified on economic grounds.*

ANALYSIS: *The concept of "environmental economics" was pioneered by Pres. George H. W. Bush, but has been rejected by the Republican Party (for example, the "cap-and-trade" policy on pp. 120-1 and "carbon reduction incentives" on pp. 56-7) Booker personalizes "internalizing environmental benefits" into an increase in property values, rather than risking voters' eyes glazing over with a discussion of theoretical economics like on the opposite page.*

Chapter Two:
Cory Booker on Economic Issues

* indicates broken promise

* indicates broken promise

Campaign Promises on Corporate Regulation

Predatory lending & unchecked avarice destabilized economy

American economic might [stands] strong on the bedrock of the American ideal: a strong, empowered and ever-growing middle class. Our platform emphasizes that a vibrant, free and fair market is essential to economic growth.

We also must pull from our highest ideals of justice and protect against those ills that destabilized our economy — like predatory lending, over-leveraged financial institutions and the unchecked avarice of the past that trumped fairness and common sense.

Source: Democratic National Convention speech, Sept. 4, 2012

KEPT PROMISE: Booker blamed banks for the 2008 financial crisis—the term "predatory lending" implies that banks attack and consumers are the victims. Booker has followed through on that point of view in his Senate actions.

ANALYSIS: Using the term "predatory lending" represents a key distinction between Democrats and Republicans in their analysis of the causes of the Great Recession — Republicans typically blamed consumers for taking on more debt than they could handle. The policy prescription from the Republican point of view is to bail out corporations, as occurred in 2008-2009. The policy prescription from the Democratic point of view is to restrict banks and corporations so such a financial crisis is less likely to recur. Booker enacts that policy, with fellow Senate Democrats, in the letter on the opposite page.

Actions Taken on Corporate Regulation

Restrict corporate use of consumer mandatory arbitration

We write to commend the Consumer Financial Protection Bureau (CFPB) for its proposed rule to limit the use of mandatory, pre-dispute ("forced") arbitration clauses in consumer financial product and service contracts. Every day, Americans across the country are forced to sign away their constitutional right to access the courts as a condition of purchasing common products and services like credit cards, checking accounts, and private student loans. To restore Americans' access to justice and hold financial institutions accountable, we strongly support the CFPB's proposal to preserve the ability of consumers to band together in class actions when seeking relief through the civil justice system.

In recent decades, companies from a broad range of industries have increasingly employed forced arbitration clauses in their service and product contracts. These clauses require a consumer to submit any claim that may arise against a company to binding arbitration — a privatized justice system that studies show consistently produces results that favor large corporations and offers no meaningful appeals process. These contract provisions also frequently include a class action waiver, meaning that consumers are unable to band together through collective action to address widespread wrongdoings by powerful corporations. Class action waivers can prevent consumers from seeking recourse altogether, because the claims are so small that consumers cannot afford to pursue them individually. As a result, consumers are left without redress, and companies are unaccountable for their unscrupulous behavior.

Arbitration clauses are included in contracts for loans, such as auto loans, credit cards, or private student loans — essential services that American families rely on every day. Armed with these clauses, banks and financial companies are able to prevent consumers from raising disputes in court individually or as a class, which might otherwise deter practices that harm consumers.

Source: Letter from 35 senators to the CFPB, Aug. 4, 2016

Campaign Promises on Corporate Partnerships

Corporate campaign donors also helped rebuild Newark

Some see Booker as "a big-shot celebrity, a man who is using the mayor's office to build his own fame and wealth." His campaigns have been underwritten by Wall Street donors, many of whom otherwise give almost solely to Republicans. Unsurprisingly, the mayor has developed a finance-friendly view of the world. This became a matter of national controversy in May, when he called the Obama campaign's attacks on Bain Capital "nauseating". Critics pointed out that Booker had received hundreds of thousands in contributions from figures at Bain and other private-equity firms.

His connections have certainly helped get Newark back on its feet. This becomes clear as we drive down Bergen Street: After the riots, it became an alley of boarded-over storefronts and vacant lots. With new business investment, the area is showing signs of life, albeit of a more suburban kind: There's an Applebee's, an AutoZone, and a multiplex, which Booker was intent on siting close to the sidewalk, to encourage pedestrian traffic.

Source: Vogue magazine profile, "Local Hero Cory Booker", Dec. 19, 2012

KEPT PROMISE: *Voters expected Booker to continue his pro-corporate agenda, and Booker has done so as a senator.*

ANALYSIS: *Many progressives would pause before making corporate deals like Booker does – and hence would be unhappy that Booker has kept this promise. But Booker had a long history as mayor of corporate deal-making – especially on schools, see pp. 98-103, but also public-private deals on everything from city parks (p. 37) to health care (p. 66). A knee-jerk anti-corporate response, common among progressives who deeply distrust corporate power, would be to label Booker as too "cozy" with corporations. Booker, in contrast, would view corporate deal-making as "good politics," benefiting both the employers and the employees and consumers involved.*

Actions Taken on Corporate Partnerships

SOAR Act: $25M for Startup Opportunity Accelerator

Sen. Cory Booker was joined by NJ Tech Meetup, Tiger Labs, and TechLaunch at a business pitch event to highlight some of New Jersey's most innovative startups and entrepreneurs. Sen. Booker discussed his recent introduction of the Startup Opportunity Accelerator, or SOAR, Act. The legislation would direct $25 million of funding over five years to a U.S. Small Business Administration program called the Growth Accelerator Fund. The program allows business startups to compete for funding to help their businesses grow.

The Growth Accelerator Fund helps companies to find new connections, new routes to investment, and new ideas and strategies to achieve their full potential. The SOAR Act also gives special consideration to applicants serving women and minority business owners.

"This program will stimulate our nation's entrepreneurial energy and spur economic growth in untapped areas," Sen. Booker said. "Over the past 17 years, the number of women-owned businesses in New Jersey has increased more than 48 percent and I'm looking forward to seeing that growth continue," Sen. Booker added. "With the SOAR Act, we'll be able to increase investments made in promising entrepreneurs, who will put their ingenuity to work for the benefit of their neighbors."

The pitch-off event held at Tiger Labs in Princeton consisted of five New Jersey startups showcasing their products before an expert panel of investors and tech leaders. The event also provided an opportunity for entrepreneurs to connect with other innovators and business leaders across New Jersey.

Source: Press Release from Senate office booker.senate.gov,
Sept. 24, 2014

Campaign Promises on Economic Justice

We will not be able to cut our way out of the jobs crisis

Too many New Jerseyans are still hurting. While the economy has started to come back from the worst economic downturn in generations, New Jersey was the last state in the country to join the jobs recovery, and we continue to lag behind. Even among those who are employed, too many are finding that jobs aren't paying like they used to. Paychecks are getting smaller and bills are piling up.

Occupations in fields such as construction and manufacturing, with median hourly wages of $13.84 to $21.13 – the middle third of the pay scale – accounted for 60 percent of job losses during the worst part of the recession. As the recovery progressed, however, those jobs didn't come back. Instead, it was lower-wage occupations – those with median hourly wages of $7.69 to $13.83 – that accounted for 58 percent of all job growth

Washington, however, doesn't seem to get it. We will not be able to cut our way out of the jobs crisis. The defeat of many aspects of President Obama's jobs plan, on the basis that it meant a short-term spending bump, is emblematic of Congress's inability to reconcile smart spending and investment now with long-term deficit reduction efforts that will help ensure our economic prosperity.

We must act to empower those who are suffering now, removing roadblocks that prevent them and their families from getting back on their feet. Doing that is about more than simply protecting the most vulnerable or those at risk of falling from the middle class into poverty. It means providing help to people who are likely to spend the extra money they have in their paychecks every month – a hand up that will create benefits throughout the economy.

Source: CoryBooker.com Senate campaign website, Nov. 3, 2013

Actions Taken on Economic Justice

Newark got disproportionate share of dumps & jails

When I was growing up in the 1980s, Newark was a place often maligned or feared in the suburbs. Mentions of the city inspired concern or even pity expressed in a way that was often insulting.

New Jersey was happy to place in Newark a state prison, a county jail, waste disposal sites, sewage treatment facilities, halfway houses, drug treatment centers. A grossly disproportionate share of public and low-income housing, and other necessary public goods that wouldn't be located in surrounding suburban towns. Despite this, Newark still boasted New Jersey's finest cultural institutions, including the state's largest public library and museum. It was the state's largest college town and it was home to massive job generators such as Newark Liberty International Airport.

There was a tenacious resolve in Newark to show the world a truth that would upset shallow assertions that Newark was dead. There was a vast communal will to demonstrate that this once great city would rise again.

Source: United, by Senator Cory Booker, p. 29-30, Feb. 16, 2016

KEPT PROMISE: *Booker has always focused on the underclass: those who are forgotten in economic policy (like in the recovery from the Great Recession, in the campaign promise to the left), or who are ignored when siting dumps and jails (like in Booker's memoir, above).*

ANALYSIS: *Themes of economic justice are the core value for progressives, who accept Booker because of his focus on this theme, despite their suspicions of his motivations on other themes. The opposing viewpoint – which Booker has never adhered to – is that the best way to help the underclass is by providing freedom to take advantage of opportunities for advancement.*

Campaign Promises on Budget Deficit

Replace spending with tax incentives to stimulate hiring

"The federal government needs to cut spending," Booker said before a packed room at Saint Anselm College. [He cited former Sen. Jack Kemp, R-NY]: "It's because we shared the same ideas. Kemp believed that if you give the right tax incentives in urban areas, you create opportunity."

Booker said Obama is introducing policies similar to Kemp's, such as tax incentives for businesses that reinvest in the economy. "Over the last 3-plus years [Obama] has cut taxes on small businesses 17 times," Booker said. "Giving businesses tax incentives to hire people coming back from Iraq and Afghanistan; ideas that to me seem like every American, regardless of your party, should stand up and embrace."

Source: Speech at Saint Anselm College (New Hampshire), Dec. 9, 2011

BACKGROUND: *The federal budget dwarfs the scale of Newark's city budget ($697 million in FY2015, Booker's last year). Scaled to the federal level, Booker's $60 million cuts cited on the opposite page were the federal equivalent of $327 billion.*

Spending in federal budget (FY2015)
$3.81 trillion total

Non-discretionary spending:
$897 billion (23%) Social Security
$860 billion (23%) Medicare/Medicaid
$251 billion (7%) interest on debt
$659 billion (17%) other mandatory
Discretionary spending:
$606 billion (16%) national defense
$543 billion (14%) other discretionary

Federal revenue sources
$1,498 billion (39%)
        income taxes
$1,055 billion (28%)
        FICA/Medicare
$ 412 billion (11%)
        corporate taxes
$ 286 billion (7%)
        other taxes
$ 565 billion (15%)
        budget deficit

Actions Taken on Budget Deficit

Budget crisis: cut $60M in spending; cut municipal taxes

So much was said when our City, in the midst of a $180 million budget crisis, moved to take aggressive corrective action. After cutting spending by $60 million and increasing revenue in a like amount, our City still faced a budget crisis of monumental proportions with mounting personnel costs.

We refused to tax our way out of this problem and did the unheard-of thing. In 2007, thanks to Municipal Council support, we cut our municipal tax rate in order to absorb tax increases by the County and for the school district so that we could sustain the same overall tax rate for our citizens.

We made the difficult decision to eliminate hundreds of job vacancies from the budget, offer buy-outs for employees to voluntarily separate and ultimately lay off 65 employees. Local government cannot be about employment, it must be about efficiency, effectiveness, about delivering the best of services to residents and dedicated to creating business and employment opportunity for residents outside of government.

Source: State of the City Address, Feb. 1, 2008

KEPT PROMISE: *We switch the timing of Booker's promise here – Booker's "Action Taken" was as mayor, years earlier than his "Campaign Promise" for what he would do as senator. We're interpreting a mayoral action as indicative of his attitude toward applying city fiscal action at the federal level.*

ANALYSIS: *Booker wants to portray himself as unwilling to accept the standard "tax-and-spend liberal" methods. As mayor, he made hard cuts, combining program cuts with layoffs and a mix of tax changes. At the federal level, he cites a Republican program with a similar mix of policies. Booker passes the test of "fiscal responsibility" here, but Booker obfuscates about taxation as badly as any irresponsible politician by pretending that "increasing revenue" by $60 million was somehow not "taxing our way out of this problem." We point this out as a broken promise on pp. 62-3; here we focus on the budgetary aspects.*

Campaign Promises on Energy Efficiency

Eliminate unfair subsidies for oil and gas

As your Senator, I will work tirelessly to ensure that the United States is a world leader in the green economy, and that we address global warming before it is too late. My priorities will include:

- Fighting to eliminate unfair and unnecessary subsidies for the oil and gas industry that put the United States at a disadvantage in the race to develop green technology;

- Opposing drilling in the waters off of the Jersey Shore;

- Working to support comprehensive climate change legislation that incentivizes the creation of green jobs and significantly reduces greenhouse gas emissions.

A healthy environment is in everyone's interest; Democrats, Republicans, and Independents all breathe the same air. As mayor I brought people together – from business, government and the community – to address local and regional environmental concerns, and will carry the same approach with me to Washington to tackle our federal challenges.

Source: CoryBooker.com Senate campaign website, Nov. 3, 2013

BACKGROUND: *Booker espouses the "No Regrets Policy," which is advocated by green energy supporters as an economically-responsible means of achieving progress on carbon reduction. "No Regrets" means advocating policies that would make sense even if your goal were NOT carbon reduction, because they save money or have other benefits. Such policies include adopting energy-efficient technology locally – such as home weatherization – which reduces consumers heating bills or electricity bills. Nationally, "No Regrets" policies include reducing fossil fuel subsidies for budget benefit; and banning off-shore drilling to reduce environmental risks.*

Actions Taken on Energy Efficiency

Weatherization of 450 homes; free for seniors

Our partnerships with La Casa de Don Pedro and First Hopewell have led to the weatherization of over 450 homes — helping residents save money with lower utility bills and creating jobs for Newarkers. We've partnered with Local 55 to train residents for jobs in weatherization, resulting in free home weatherization for dozens of our seniors. And we are moving forward with the sale of city-owned, abandoned homes to small, local contractors who will work with Local 55 to rehabilitate and weatherize them.

Source: State of the City Address at Newark Symphony Hall, Feb. 9, 2010

KEPT PROMISE: *Booker prefers "No Regrets" policies as a moderate alternative rather than a hard-core direct tax on carbon usage. He has avoided using terms like "carbon tax" — see pp. 56-57 — but his goals are the same as those who advocate a carbon tax: a shift away from fossil fuel and towards greener fuel sources. Booker promises that his policies would "significantly reduce greenhouse gas emissions" – that is possible with "No Regrets" policies, but it is the same language as used by hard-core advocates who mean "subsidize green energy" or "tax gas and oil" or both. A careful reading of Booker's promises and actions indicates that, yes, he would PARTICIPATE in "comprehensive climate change legislation," but he would ADVOCATE only for moderate "No Regrets" policies that would not directly take on the fossil fuel industry.*

ANALYSIS: *The alternative to the "No Regrets" policy is the "All-of-the-Above" policy, in which the candidate claims support of all sources of energy, for the purpose of reducing energy imports or boosting the economy. Booker does not subscribe to an the "All-of-the-Above" policy – he supports nuclear energy (next page) but NOT oil/gas/coal energy (opposite page). An example of a Republican citing "All-of-the-Above" appears on the opposite page – it's the conservative rationale for nuclear power (but not Booker's rationale). "All-of-the-Above" really means "support the perpetuation of the oil, gas, and coal industries," with some lip-service to nuclear power and renewable energy.*

Campaign Promises on Nuclear Power

Support existing nuclear power by pricing carbon

Alarmed by the growing number of US nuclear power plants that have closed or might soon close because of cheap, abundant natural gas, industry officials are calling for speedy government action to rebalance an electricity market that they say is stacked against them.

Replacing all the shuttered plants with new natural-gas generation would wipe out about one-quarter of the carbon emissions reductions that are projected in the administration's Clean Power Plan. The changeover would also cancel out 40% of the cuts to greenhouse gas emissions that the US committed to in December at the Paris climate change conference.

"We've got to support the existing nuclear fleet," said Senator Cory Booker (D-NJ). "We must make a goal of passing a law that establishes an economy-wide price on carbon to allow nuclear to compete on a level playing field."

Electricity markets have failed to give nuclear energy credit for being a clean, zero-carbon source that has provided around-the-clock, base-load power. To encourage the growth of wind and solar energy, Congress has subsidized them with 30% production tax credits. But because they are intermittent sources and there are currently no reliable energy storage systems, neither is as dependable as nuclear or coal. Nuclear's ongoing, seemingly intractable waste-disposal issue was not discussed, nor was the public's uneasiness with the technology.

Source: Physics Today, "Decline of US nuclear industry," June 1, 2016

KEPT PROMISE: *Booker made no secret of his support for nuclear power during his campaigns. He paired that policy with carbon reduction (the liberal view) instead of focusing on domestic energy production or cheap energy for the economy (the conservative view). He maintains that policy preference even when collaborating on legislation with Republicans who prefer the more conservative focus.*

Actions Taken on Nuclear Power

Federal collaboration for advanced nuclear technologies

The U.S. Senate today approved overwhelmingly legislation that would increase collaboration among private industry, universities, and national laboratories to facilitate the development of advanced nuclear technologies. The vote of 87 to 4 to approve the amendment makes it a part of a larger energy policy reform bill before the Senate.

The Nuclear Energy Innovation Capabilities Act (NEICA), S. 2461, directs the U.S. Department of Energy (DOE) to prioritize partnering with private innovators on new reactor technologies and the testing and demonstration of reactor concepts.

"Nuclear energy has an important role to play as we transition to a carbon-free energy future. This amendment will help drive investment, remove bureaucratic barriers, and allow our entrepreneurs and businesses to unleash the promise of advanced nuclear technologies," said Booker.

"Including clean nuclear energy as part of our nation's 'all-of-the-above' energy strategy is a no-brainer," said Senator Jim Risch (R-ID).

"I am pleased to join this bipartisan group in supporting nuclear energy development, which is crucial to our economy," Senator Orrin Hatch (R-UT) said.

Source: Press Release from 5 senators on Nuclear Energy Legislation, Jan. 28, 2016

*ANALYSIS: The last new nuclear plant to come on-line in the US was in 1996, due to both political and economic issues. Pres. Obama promoted new nuclear plants as part of a comprehensive energy plan; the NRC accordingly approved a new nuclear plant design in Dec. 2011, the first in decades. The **nuclear renaissance** is now underway, with the start of construction of four new plants to add to the 100 existing reactors. Congress must soon deal with the key remaining issue: what to do with nuclear waste. The current plan is to bury it all at **Yucca Mountain** in the Nevada desert; ongoing lawsuits are continuing.*

Campaign Promises on Carbon Tax

Has never taken a public position on a carbon tax

[Booker's opponent Rep. Rush] Holt launched his first TV ad and faulted Booker for not supporting a carbon tax or breaking up large banking institutions in the 31-second spot. "Cory Booker may be the frontrunner in this race, but he's not progressive," Holt said in the ad running until the election on broadcast in NYC and cable in Philadelphia.

A Booker campaign spokesman questioned the ad's validity, saying the mayor has never taken a public position on a carbon tax or breaking up banks. "It's disappointing that Representative Holt would mislead voters about Mayor Booker's record," he said.

Source: Wall Street Journal coverage of 2013 N.J. Senate debate, Aug. 5, 2013

Create green economy with lower carbon output

I endorsed Senator Obama [for president] because he is committed to strengthening the federal commitment to our cities through several key initiatives, including creating a new green economy, which will not only lower carbon output, increase energy efficiency, and reduce our dependence on foreign oil but also create new businesses and tens of thousands of new jobs.

Source: Cory Booker column on Huffington Post, Nov. 4, 2008

BROKEN PROMISE: *The Booker campaign claimed that Booker had never supported a carbon tax, but in fact he had supported "lower carbon output." Voters would infer from his support of "lower carbon output" that Booker would support some sort of economic incentive to achieve that. We call that a broken promise by "**legalism**."*

ANALYSIS: *Booker was TECHNICALLY not lying when he said he never supported a carbon TAX – he meant he supported OTHER forms of economic incentives (paid for with taxes, of course) – but he omitted that from his campaign explanation, even when given the chance to clarify. That omission misled voters into thinking he opposed incentives for reducing carbon output. And he DID support reducing carbon output in his actions in the Senate, in contradiction to his misleading omission.*

Actions Taken on Carbon Tax

50% clean and carbon free electricity by 2030

Booker co-sponsored H.Res.637/S.Res.386, expressing the sense of Congress that the United States should establish a national goal of more than 50 percent clean and carbon free electricity by 2030 for the purposes of avoiding the worst impacts of climate change, growing our economy, increasing our shared prosperity, improving public health, and preserving our national security.

- Whereas failing to act on climate change will have a devastating impact on our Nation's economy, costing us billions of dollars in lost GDP;

- Whereas extreme weather, intensified by climate change, has already cost taxpayers billions of dollars each year in recovery efforts, and this will only continue if climate change is left unaddressed;

- Whereas inaction on climate change will disproportionately impact communities of color and exacerbate existing economic inequalities;

- Whereas the transition to a clean energy economy is feasible with existing technology;

- Whereas the transition to clean energy will create millions of jobs and will increase our country's GDP and increase disposable household income;

- Resolved, That it is the sense of Congress that the United States should —

- Establish a national goal of more than 50 percent clean and carbon free electricity by 2030; and

- Enact legislation to accelerate the transition to clean energy to meet this goal.

Source: Resolution for 50% Carbon-Free Electricity by 2030, S.Res.386 on March 3, 2016

Campaign Promises on Campaign Finance Reform

Make it difficult for wealthy to influence politicians

[Accomplishments as City Councilor toward] Better Government:

- Campaign Finance Reform: Wrote systematic campaign finance reform legislation, making it more difficult for wealthy contractors to influence politicians.
- Council Spending Reform: Passed legislation restricting council spending, mandating council expenditures be voted on in public meetings.
- Perk and Pay Raise Reform: Fought to end perks and pay raises for politicians, and voted against all pay raises.
- Turned down municipal car and advocated for others to do the same.
- Eliminated the use of expense accounts for personal meals or travel.
- Fought to institute performance-based budgeting, creating more accountable department management.

Source: CoryBooker.com Mayoral campaign website, Feb. 7, 2002

Campaign PACs shouldn't speak louder than people

Booker tried to distinguish the differences between Democrats and Republicans: "To me no side has a monopoly on good ideas, but when I look at this [2012 GOP] platform, in many ways it's gotten a lot more extreme than even past Republican platforms and that's very disturbing to me," Booker said. "Take campaign finance reform — for crying out loud, I mean this is incredible. This platform says pull back even more of the rules on campaign finance reform, get rid of McCain-Feingold," Booker, a co-chair on the Democratic platform committee, said. "This platform says well, wait a minute, we're out of control right now with all this super PAC money, we want to find a way to put more fair rules on campaign finance reform so that money doesn't speak louder than people. And so that to me is very dramatic."

Source: Politifact.com FactCheck on N.J. Senate race, Sept. 5, 2012

Actions Taken on Campaign Finance Reform

Matching fund for small donors; require debates

Booker sponsored the Senate Campaign Disclosure Parity Act. Congressional Summary: Fair Elections Now Act — Amends 1971 FECA:

- 500% matching payments to candidates for certain small dollar contributions;
- a public debate requirement;
- establishment of the Fair Elections Fund and of a Fair Elections Oversight Board;
- remission to the Fair Elections Fund of unspent funds after an election, civil penalties for violation of contribution and expenditure requirements;
- requires all designations, statements, and reports required to be filed under FECA to be filed directly with the FEC in electronic form accessible by computers.

Statement of support: (Sunlight Foundation) Now we bring you the Senate Campaign Disclosure Parity Act, a bill that should probably be the least controversial of all. S. 375 would simply require senators and Senate candidates to file their public campaign finance disclosure reports electronically with the Federal Election Commission, the way House candidates and presidential candidates have been filing for over a decade. A version of the bill has been introduced during every congress starting in 2003 (!) yet it has been blocked repeatedly, a victim of political football.

Source: S375/H.R.269 14_S375 on Feb. 25, 2013

KEPT PROMISE: Booker is a hard-core progressive on campaign finance and on all related "clean election" and "clean government" issues.

ANALYSIS: Booker turned down the normal benefits of mayoral office – which his opponents derided as "publicity stunts" but which his supporters described as "putting your money where your mouth is." Booker has taken this attitude to the Senate, where he further delighted progressives by tying campaign finance reform to mandatory campaign debates, another progressive dream.

Campaign Promises on Business Taxation

Lower corporate tax rate & close loopholes

Our corporate tax code offers a veritable menu of misplaced incentives and a high tax rate. But there is an alternative. Together, we can create a simple, dependable tax code that levels the playing field, creates jobs, and positions American businesses to lead the world. Any eventual solution should include the following:

- *Lowering the corporate tax rate:* We must streamline the tax code and lower the statutory corporate rate, which at about 40% is the highest among all peer countries. [We should] reduce the corporate tax rate to near 28%.

- *Eliminating misdirected corporate loopholes:* The U.S. corporate tax code is teeming with tax breaks, loopholes, and exemptions. Companies take advantage of these special carve-outs to pay much less than the official corporate tax rate — and often pay nothing at all.

Under our current system, these practices may be perfectly legal, but they aren't fair.

Source: CoryBooker.com Senate campaign website, July 1, 2014

Attacks on private equity "nauseating"

What Booker's critics mainly take issue with are his associations. Exhibit A is always Booker's notorious appearance on *Meet the Press* in May 2012, in which he called the Obama campaign's attacks on private equity "nauseating" and pleaded for more civility in the campaign. Booker subsequently clarified that he supported the specific critiques of Mitt Romney's record, but for some liberals, the betrayal was irreversible.

Booker has, it is true, raised plenty of money from Wall Street. Of the $8.6 million he's raised for his Senate campaign, $531,000 came from the financial industry. This is hardly unique for a Democrat from New Jersey, where many financial firms are headquartered.

Source: The Atlantic, "Why Do Liberals Hate Booker?" by Molly Ball, Aug. 23, 2013

Actions Taken on Business Taxation

One-time building sale, plus tax increase,
to balance budget

By making the difficult decisions this year — involving layoffs, reductions in spending across the board, and a tax increase — Newark will be fully able to operate under the 2% property tax cap advocated for by the mayor and implemented by the State Legislature. In other words, Newark has difficult choices to make today in order to insure its long-term fiscal strength and success.

The balanced budget originally presented by the mayor was no longer feasible. The City is pursuing another option to avoid a seriously damaging tax increase: a sale/leaseback of certain municipal buildings. This plan is projected to cut the remaining budget gap by 53%, and it will also provide much-needed funds to improve several city buildings. Governments across the country have pursued this option as they face similar struggles. This one-time revenue combined with other measures will significantly temper the required increase; however, some tax increase will still be required.

Source: Introduced Budget: Mayor's Commentary Press Release, Feb. 9, 2010

KEPT PROMISE: Progressives might not like it, but Booker followed through on his promises. Booker has always been open about his affinity for working with business, and in his mayoral fiscal crisis, he prioritized taxing homes and selling assets, rather than taxing businesses.

ANALYSIS: Booker believes in collaborating with businesses: they reward him with campaign donations; he returns the favor with pro-business tax policy and pro-business sentiments in the press. Booker's progressive critics are suspicious of that cozy relationship, but Booker has demonstrated that, first, he advocates pro-business policies only if they also help workers (like a property tax cap that benefits businesses as well as homeowners); and that second, he has proven immune to the secretive back-room deals that plague other pro-business politicians (in line with his open government stances).

Campaign Promises on Tax Reform

No tax increases; no pay raises; no City perks

[Accomplishments on City Council for] Better Government:

- Right to Speak Reform: Championed the effort to restore citizens' right to speak before the City Council.

- Voted against all pay raises.

- Performance-Based Budgeting: Fought to institute performance-based budgeting, creating more accountable department management.

- Streamline Budget Process: Worked to reform and streamline the budget process.

- No Tax Increases: Voted against mayor's tax increases.

Source: CoryBooker.com Mayoral campaign website, Feb. 7, 2002

BROKEN PROMISE: *Booker said "no tax increases" in 2002 and meant "I opposed THAT tax increase" but voters interpreted it as "no tax increases in the future." We call that a "**legalism,**" pretending that there is a meaningful difference. He broke his no-tax promise as mayor, and went on to adopt more pro-tax rhetoric in the Senate.*

ANALYSIS: *President George H. W. Bush lost his 1992 re-election in large part due to breaking his "no new taxes" pledge. Booker should have learned the lesson of absolute no-tax pledges; he ignored that lesson for political expediency in 2002.*

Actions Taken on Tax Reform

Raise taxes because quick fix of cuts wasn't enough

Q: Is it time to raise taxes in Newark?

A: Well, look, unfortunately we've had to, but to me, I always say we're a slave to the tyranny of a quick fix. Unfortunately, whether it's at the federal level or the local level, you just can't get out of the problems we have dug ourselves into by one solution or the other. So what do we do in Newark? We cut the size of our government by nearly 20% of our employees. We have made very dramatic cuts into overall government, because that just has to be done. But in addition to that, we have also raised taxes because the problems that we are in could not be gotten out of by one solution. There's no one trick to this. You have to have a comprehensive strategy to attack these issues.

Source: Neal Conan on National Public Radio's Talk of the Nation, July 21, 2011

Paying your fair share isn't class warfare, it's patriotism

Our platform calls for significant cuts in federal spending. Our platform calls for a balanced deficit reduction plan where the wealthy pay their fair share.

This platform is a clear choice between economic pathways: forward or back, inclusion or exclusion, grow together as a nation or be a country of savage disparities that favor the fortunate few over the greatest driving force of any economy — a large and robust middle class.

And when your country is in a costly war, with our soldiers sacrificing abroad and our nation facing a debt crisis at home, being asked to pay your fair share isn't class warfare — it's patriotism.

We choose forward. We choose inclusion. We choose growing together. We choose American economic might and muscle, standing strong on the bedrock of the American ideal: a strong, empowered and ever-growing middle class.

Source: Democratic National Convention speech, Sept. 4, 2012

Campaign Promises on ObamaCare

ObamaCare needs to be improved, but is helping people now

Booker applauded Obama's Affordable Care Act — better known as "ObamaCare" — and chastised Republicans in Washington for fighting it to the point of forcing a partial shutdown of the federal government. He said the health care overhaul is helping people who have children with diseases that would have been denied coverage under the old system. "ObamaCare needs to be improved, and what we should be doing in Washington is working together (on it)," Booker said. "These are real people's lives."

Source: Newark Star-Ledger coverage of N.J. Senate debate, Oct. 5, 2013

ObamaCare is a vital step in the right direction

- Health care costs are a factor in over 60 percent of bankruptcies;

- Millions of Americans exhaust their savings every year trying to cover medical expenses;

- Many people without insurance have been unable to get treatment.

This is unacceptable, and I firmly support the Affordable Care Act as a vital step in the right direction. I believe that the ACA has begun, and will continue, to significantly transform our health care landscape. For example, right here in New Jersey, the Affordable Care Act has closed the Medicare donut hole for 109,000 Medicare beneficiaries and will save middle class New Jerseyans more than $1,000 per year by 2019.

In Newark, we know that investing up front can produce great gains in the long run, and that the opposite is equally and sadly true. As mayor I did not wait for the federal government to improve health access for Newarkers.

Source: CoryBooker.com Senate campaign website, Nov. 3, 2013

Actions Taken on ObamaCare

Repealing ObamaCare hurts working-class

TAPPER: You have been very critical of the Republican approach to repealing and replacing Obamacare. Don't Democrats have an obligation to help fix this bill?

BOOKER: Well, clearly, that would be great if they were coming with open hearts and saying, "Hey, this is not perfect, let's fix it." Now, let's be clear. Even before the Affordable Care Act, I was the mayor of a city dealing with health care costs. They were going up significantly. So don't put this all on this ACA. I don't think you will find a Democrat or a Republican in the Senate who wouldn't honestly tell you that things weren't perfect before. And what we're saying in the Democratic Party is, "Let's build upon it, let's fix it."

TAPPER: Republicans are going to repeal and replace Obamacare. It's happening. Don't you, as a member of the Senate, have an obligation to get in there, join them, and try to improve the bill?

BOOKER: Well, I mean, that's really where we are. The Republicans cannot just force this down our throats. It's going to knock a lot of folks off, hurt long-term care, hurt good working-class folks. Their political strategy is bad politics. But, deeper than that, it is bad policy and bad process.

Source: CNN "State of the Union" with Jake Tapper, March 12, 2017

KEPT PROMISE: *Booker was a solid supporter of ObamaCare om the campaign trail, and is a solid supporter of ObamaCare in the Republican Senate's process of repealing and replacing it. Booker has taken his characteristically cautious wording in support of SOME parts of ObamaCare, while making sure to point out that reforming OTHER parts are ok.*

ANALYSIS: *Note Booker's description of ObamaCare as "a step in the right direction" – progressives use that phrase to mean "ObamaCare is a step toward single-payer." Booker instead means something like "a step in the right direction of affordable health insurance." For progressives, healthcare is a social justice issue; for Booker, it is an economic issue – both in his campaign promises and in his Senate actions.*

Campaign Promises on Single-Payer

Control healthcare cost; no comment on single-payer

One of the most contentious parts [of the Democratic primary debate for the special election for Senate] was over health insurance.

- N.J. House Speaker Sheila Oliver and Democratic U.S. Rep. [Frank] Pallone said they support a government-run insurance system but that it can't get passed now.

- Democratic U.S. Rep. Rush Holt told them that their approach is "another way of saying we can only do things that we clear with the Tea Party."

- Mayor Booker called for controlling health care costs but avoided the single-payer debate.

Source: Politico.com coverage of N.J. Senate debate, Aug. 6, 2013

We need a national solution and also local solutions

More recently dealing with health care crisis, people are saying we've got to find a national solution. I agree with that. But we've been finding local solutions.

Source: Interview at Fairfield University by News 64, Feb. 21, 2009

Newark Rx: affordable medications for uninsured

The health care challenges of Newark and all American cities will continue until federal action is taken, but we will not take this challenge lying down and today we acknowledge a win in the battle for health care justice in Newark.

I am truly pleased tonight to announce Newark Rx, to begin to combat the rising costs of prescription drugs. Newark Rx will create immediate access to affordable medications for thousands of uninsured Newark residents. Newark Rx is the creation of my office, Heinz Family Philanthropies, PhRMA, and other innovative partners.

Source: State of the City Address at Newark Symphony Hall, Feb. 9, 2009

Actions Taken on Single-Payer

Ok to consider single-payer, but I'm not behind it

During Barack Obama's presidency, Rep. John Conyers (D-MI) could only find 62 other House Democrats willing to co-sponsor his single-payer health care proposal — which would expand Medicare to cover every American. But now that Speaker Paul Ryan's House health care bill has imploded, Conyers's team has already signed up 78 co-sponsors for the exact same single-payer bill. And Sen. Bernie Sanders announced over the weekend he'd be launching a new Medicare-for-All initiative.

But while Sanders and progressive Democrats clamor for a more aggressive approach, some Senate Democrats expressed skepticism about the need to go that far, that quickly.

Sen. Cory Booker (D-NJ) wouldn't get behind a single-payer health care system, instead calling it "one of those options that must be considered" in an email to Vox. Sen. Claire McCaskill (D-MO) was openly critical, arguing "it's important that we keep options open for people who rely on health care." Most preferred to duck the question altogether, and concentrate on defending Americans who are covered under Obamacare, as Sen. Bob Casey (D-PA) put it.

Source: Jeff Stein in Vox.com, "TrumpCare dead," March 29, 2017

BACKGROUND: *'Single Payer' refers to replacing private insurance companies with federal or state payments to hospitals and doctors. The 'public option' in ObamaCare would have been a voluntary opt-in to single-payer, but single-payer was never part of ObamaCare. Medicare-for-All is another means of implementing single-payer healthcare.*

BROKEN PROMISE: *Saying 'No comment' under direct questioning is a particularly misleading way to **muddy-the-water**.*

ANALYSIS: *Of course Booker had an opinion at that time — but Booker did not want to SAY that he opposed single-payer, because progressives prefer single-payer. So he let voters hope that he supported it OR that he opposed it, depending on their preference — a good way to get votes, but a bad way to be honest. When it came to co-sponsoring a single-payer bill, Booker declined, demonstrating what he believed all along, and was unwilling to tell the public.*

Campaign Promises on Union Policy

Held over 100 Job Fairs to employ local residents

[Accomplishments on City Council on] Jobs and Economic Opportunity:

- **First Source Legislation:** Passed comprehensive first source legislation mandating that companies in Newark look to hire Newark residents first before hiring those that live outside of the city.

- **Job Fairs:** Held over 100 Job Fairs with area businesses to employ local residents.

- **Jobs for City Youth:** Fought for more summer jobs for city youth including putting a program in the budget for a youth employment program.

Source: CoryBooker.com Mayoral campaign website, Feb. 7, 2002

*BROKEN PROMISE: Booker studiously said nothing about his relations with unions during his mayoral campaign and Senate campaign, which is the same type of **muddy-the-water** lie as "no comment" except that no debate moderator directly asked him. The three job-based accomplishments above all SOUND vaguely pro-union – or they sound vaguely anti-union – depending on what each voter preferred. Booker could not win on our Promise Kept scale if he's that vague – no matter what he later did, we would rate it as a **muddy-the-water** broken promise.*

ANALYSIS: Booker's actual actions make it clear WHY he was vague: he is generally in favor of union organizing, but has a long antagonistic record with teachers' unions due to his pro-charter school stance (see pp. 100-1). By avoiding union issues, the teachers' union would not have the opportunity to denounce Booker. Booker took plenty of heat for his pro-charter stance – but he was honest about that! He would have taken even more heat if he publicly made the connection – like many Democrats and liberals do — between a pro-charter stance and an anti-union stance.

Actions Taken on Union Policy

Urban school districts are beholden to public unions

[In a joint tour of Newark during Chris Christie's gubernatorial campaign], Booker proposed to Christie that they work together to transform education in Newark. Together, they could close failing district schools, greatly expand charter schools, and weaken tenure protections — an agenda the incumbent Democratic governor, Jon Corzine, likely never would have embraced, out of loyalty to teachers' unions. Christie's upset victory over Corzine, in Booker's view, represented "a once-in-a-lifetime chance to get the system on the right track."

Booker warned that they would face a brutal fight with unions and machine politicians invested in the status quo. Whatever their political differences, Booker and Christie agreed completely on public education. Both viewed urban school districts as beholden to public workers' unions and political patronage rather than children.

Source: The Prize: Who's In Charge of America's Schools?
by Dale Russakoff, pp. 5-6, Sept. 8, 2015

Let Senate cafeteria workers organize their own union

Employees working full time in the U.S. Senate should not be living in poverty. Yet with the cost of living in Washington, there have been numerous reports of Senate cafeteria workers forced to take a second job, and rely on public assistance programs.

[The workers are currently pushing for a union through the majority sign up process, but the Compass Group, the employer of Senate dining workers, has resisted the drive, even after the National Labor Relations Board upheld charges against the company regarding discriminatory and intimidating behavior.] Although the Compass Group settled these charges by promising to end further unlawful intimidation, the Compass Group has discouraged their organizing campaign.

We request that the Compass Group commit to reaching an agreement with the union seeking to organize these workers, and recognize the union as the worker's exclusive bargaining representative on the basis of majority representation of signed authorization cards.

Source: Letter from 31 senators to the Compass Group, Nov. 13, 2015

Campaign Promises on Minimum Wage

Passed laws on prevailing wage & large-scale firings

Our Administration has taken numerous steps [on labor issues]: from being the first city in New Jersey to adopt a prevailing wage law to the first city to pass legislation to prevent large scale firing of workers when new contracts are awarded.

Source: State of the City Address, Feb. 1, 2008

Fair wage jumpstarts consumer spending & creates jobs

Senator Booker believes that anyone who is willing to work hard and play by the rules should be able to succeed in America. Senator Booker supports raising the minimum wage because he knows that when a family is able to earn a fair wage, they are able to create a more stable and healthier living environment for their children, to invest in our national economy, and to be involved in their communities.

Raising the minimum wage could cut the number of Americans living in poverty, jumpstart consumer spending and create jobs.

Source: Senate website, booker.senate.gov, "Issues", April 1, 2017

BACKGROUND: *The federal minimum wage is currently $7.25, increased from $5.15 in 2009, by an act of Congress. The last increase took place in three stages over a period of years; another increase will require another act of Congress. Some candidates want to increase it again now, and automatically increase it to keep up with inflation (known as "indexing"). President Obama has proposed (and as of 2016, some states have already adopted) a new minimum wage of $10.10 per hour. Laws on "prevailing wage" are a means to ensure local minimum wage increase, typically in urban areas with higher costs of living.*

Actions Taken on Minimum Wage

Raise the minimum wage to $10.10 per hour by 2016

Booker co-sponsored the Minimum Wage Fairness Act of 2014; Congressional summary: Increases the federal minimum wage for employees to:

- $8.20 an hour beginning 6 months after enactment
- $9.15 an hour beginning 1 year later,
- $10.10 an hour beginning 2 years later, and
- an amount determined by increases in the Consumer Price Index, beginning annually after 3 years.
- Increases the federal minimum wage for tipped employees to $3.00 an hour beginning 6 months after enactment, with annual CPI adjustments.

Proponent's argument in favor (RaiseTheMinimumWage.com): The federal minimum wage of $7.25 per hour remains decades out of date, and the federal minimum wage for tipped workers — $2.13 per hour — has not increased in over 20 years. The minimum wage of the past provided significantly more buying power than it does today. The minimum wage of $1.60 an hour in 1968 would be $10.56 today when adjusted for inflation.

Opponent's argument against: (*Wall Street Journal*): The CBO concluded that a jump in the minimum wage to $10.10 an hour could eliminate 500,000 jobs. Democrats pointed to the CBO's findings that the higher wage would lift 900,000 people out of poverty. But both sides missed a key finding: That a smaller hike to $9.00 an hour would cause almost no pain, and still lift 300,000 people out of poverty.

Source: S.1737 & H.R.1010 on Nov. 19, 2013

KEPT PROMISE: *Mayor Booker supported increases in the minimum wage at the city and state level; Senator Booker supported increases in the minimum wage at the federal level.*

ANALYSIS: *Booker's attention to prevailing wage, CPI increases, and tipped-wage increases indicates full support of all aspects of the minimum wage.*

Campaign Promises on Social Security

Don't raise retirement age, except maybe young workers

Booker has been deemed suspicious when it comes to entitlement reform. The sole concrete criticism was Booker "hinting that he'd be open to raising the Social Security retirement age for young people — before backtracking furiously when progressives called him on it." Booker had been paraphrased in the *Bergen Record* as saying that he "opposes raising the retirement age for most people in the country — except, perhaps, for people in their 20s or younger." When the vagueness of that position prompted furious criticism, Booker tweeted that he opposes all cuts to Social Security and Medicare; would, if anything, expand the programs; and also opposes raising the retirement age and curbing benefits through the "chained CPI" inflation index.

But the case against Booker seems to rest chiefly on tone and approach. It seems clear Booker will not be riding to Washington on a wave of esteem from national progressives.

Source: The Atlantic, "Why Do Liberals Hate Booker?" by Molly Ball, Aug. 23, 2013

BROKEN PROMISE: *Booker's campaign "hint" was followed by repeated retractions – i.e. he learned his lesson and has taken a hard-line against all discussions of reforms ever since. We rate this an "**evolution**" because Booker has now kept up that hard line for years.*

ANALYSIS: *The story above indicates why politicians maintain vague **muddy-the-water** stances: because when they say the truth, they are criticized from one side or the other. Booker touched "the third rail" with his truthful sentiments on Social Security – that he believed that reforms might apply to younger workers. That's called "the third rail" of politics because, like a railroad's third rail, if you touch it, you die. President George W. Bush made Social Security reform a valid topic for discussion, in his rhetoric of the early 2000s, but that only defused the third rail for Republicans. For Democrats like Booker, reforms are still something not even to be discussed – and Booker has paid the price for his honest indiscretion.*

Actions Taken on Social Security

Opposes raising retirement age; expand entitlements

Cory Booker said he supports expanding Social Security and Medicare, following a press conference where his opponents challenged Booker on the issue. The Progressive Change Campaign Committee held a morning rally in Trenton with Booker's opponents pressing Booker on the Social Security issue. Later Booker took to Twitter to say that he wants to expand, not cut Social Security and Medicare, and that he opposes raising the retirement age. A week ago Booker said that he would consider voting to raise the retirement age for those in their 20s or younger.

In response to the PCCC, Booker said that he believes that tying Social Security benefits to the Consumer Price Index or a change in the retirement age would constitute cuts to the program. Booker has found himself pressed by his opponents on the Social Security issue in recent weeks, [based on] the mayor's ties to Wall Street interests. Booker has long been a recipient of campaign contributions from those in the financial services sector.

Source: Huffington Post on New Jersey Senate race, Aug. 1, 2013

COLA adjustments needed for retirement plans

Senator Booker is working to ensure that the promise of Social Security Is preserved for generations to come. He understands the vital role that Social Security plays in the lives of many New Jerseyans and knows that Social Security is an absolutely essential cornerstone of Americans' retirement plans. Senator Booker signed on as a cosponsor of the Seniors and Veterans Emergency (SAVE) Benefits Act of 2015, which would help address the lack of a cost-of-living adjustment for Americans in 2016.

Senator Booker is also fighting to make saving for retirement easier and ensure that Americans' retirement savings are not depleted by unnecessary fees and bad advice.

Source: Senate website, booker.senate.gov, "Issues", April 1, 2017

Campaign Promises on Earned Income Tax Credit

Increase EITC collections with public-private partnerships

Q: What does mayoral experience bring to the U.S. Senate?

BOOKER: I'm going to be running around our state finding very substantive pragmatic ways to make change. And there are implications to federal policy. For example, New Jersey does not do a great job collecting its earned income tax credit money. Now, this is a federal program that I'm going to be fighting for, that I have experienced in Newark significantly increasing the EITC collections by doing public-private partnerships with local grassroots activists to set up free tax center. In fact, we set one up in the basement of city hall. And so, as a mayor, I know the urgencies of the moment and how it reflects to changing federal policies, whether it is common sense background checks, whether is if how program like the EITC or child tax care credits actually make a difference for working families.

Source: Interview on MSNBC's Rachel Maddow Show, Oct. 22, 2013

BACKGROUND: The Earned Income Tax Credit (EITC) is a wage subsidy which is highly regarded — among Democrats and Republican alike — in part because it encourages work. The benefit rises with earnings until it reaches a plateau, then gradually phases out as earnings continue to rise. The EITC lifts about 6 million Americans out of poverty per year. About half of them are children.

KEPT PROMISE: Booker kept this promise with actions taken as mayor, and he has pushed for expanding the EITC as senator, too.

ANALYSIS: Booker applies his standard "public-private partnership" to this issue, but it's not controversial in this case because at the local level, the EITC is a bipartisan issue. Booker supports the EITC in Senate legislation – where it does not have bipartisan support. Hence Booker shows sincere support for continuing with this issue in the Senate.

Actions Taken on Earned Income Tax Credit

Assist beneficiaries with earned income tax credit

We aggressively stepped up our work with the earned income tax credit, even establishing a free tax center in City Hall, leading to savings of hundreds of thousands of dollars in filing fees and assisting in putting millions of previously unclaimed dollars into the pockets of residents. And now with the governor's expansion of eligibility for the state EITC, hundreds, if not thousands, more Newarkers can claim additional benefits.

Source: State of the City Address, Feb. 1, 2008

Expand EITC to more families & to job grants

Sens. Cory Booker and Tammy Baldwin introduced the Stronger Way Act, bold legislation to fight poverty in America with real solutions. Said Senator Booker, "This legislation will expand economic opportunity and keep Americans out of poverty by strengthening tax credits for working families and programs that ease the transition from unemployment to work."

The Stronger Way Act establishes a new transitional jobs grant program. This will build a new federal partnership with state and local governments, businesses, and non-profit organizations.

The Stronger Way Act increases the rate at which the Earned Income Tax Credit phases in for working families with children to both encourage work and target additional dollars to low-income working families. Workers with earnings above 50% of the poverty line receive the maximum EITC. This tax reform would reward work and benefit 63 million people, including nearly 29 million children of working parents. Currently, a childless adult working full-time and earning minimum wage receives little to no Earned Income Tax Credit and can be taxed into poverty. We need to make work pay for everyone by extending this tax credit to workers without children.

Source: Joint press release from Sen. Tammy Baldwin (D-WI)
and Sen. Booker, July 15, 2016

Post-WWII policy of redlining
forced racially-biased housing

After World War II, racially focused housing policies were set in place at every level of government — and many of them are still on the books. These policies included local restrictive covenants that banned the transfer of property to blacks, real-estate agents steering minorities away from white towns, zoning rules that allowed towns to avoid having low-income housing, overtly discriminatory mortgage lending, redlining that effectively walled minority communities off from opportunity and investment, and FHA policies that rewarded financial institutions and builders who invested in white communities.

HUD polices were put in place that directed the building of densely clustered low-income and public housing into urban spaces. Newark's nickname, "Brick City," is derived from the federal policy to pack low-income housing into Newark and not diffusely throughout the state of New Jersey, where the impact of poverty on families would have been mitigated.

Source: United, by Senator Cory Booker, p.105-6, Feb. 16, 2016

Resided in housing projects, to help tenants

Long before he became America's most influential mayor, Booker began his career as an exercise in self-imposed humility. At the age of 28, with prestigious clerkships and six-figure salaries on the horizon, he moved into a "penthouse apartment" in Brick Towers, one of Newark's worst housing projects, with the aim of helping tenants.

Booker lived there for eight years, through winters without heat or hot water, often walking up and down the fifteen flights of stairs when the elevator wasn't working. Gayle King, the CBS morning-news anchor who has become a close friend, says that by the time she started visiting him there a few years later, he no longer noticed the smell of urine in the hallways.

Source: Vogue magazine profile, "Local Hero Cory Booker", Dec. 19, 2012

Actions Taken on Housing & Homelessness

Force landlords to provide heat to residents

Accomplishments in City Council on Housing:

- Heat Legislation: (2/7/01) Passed legislation giving the city greater powers to force landlords to provide heat to residents.

- Quality Housing: (3/17/99, 4/5/00) Organized and supported dozens of tenant groups to ensure quality housing.

- Legal Support: Organized local pro-bono attorneys to provide legal support to tenant groups.

- City Code Enforcement: Advocated to enforce of city codes and for an increase in city prosecutors specifically to force landlords to comply with city codes

- Housing Conference: Organized a citywide housing conference to empower tenants and equip them with the tools and information they need.

Source: CoryBooker.com Mayoral campaign website, Feb. 7, 2002

KEPT PROMISE: We switched the timing of Booker's promises for the Senate with his actions as city councilor and mayor, because his real results were in Newark. That's not surprising, since housing and homelessness issues are much more relevant at the state and local level than at the federal level. His promises and his actions agree, overall.

ANALYSIS: Booker's rhetoric on the injustices of red-lining is classically progressive and pro-civil rights ("Red-lining" refers to real estate agencies drawing red lines on city maps, where whites live on one side, and blacks on the other side of the line). Booker's critics label as another "publicity stunt" his personally moving into the projects – but his supporters claim he now "gets it" on housing issues.

Chapter Three:
Cory Booker on Social Issues

* indicates broken promise

Campaign Promises on Abortion

No restrictions before viability; exceptions after viability

Cory Booker supports a woman's right to choose, according to his campaign website. But to hear a conservative group's ad tell it, Booker supports much more than choice.

The American Commitment Action Fund, a conservative PAC behind the BookerFAIL website, funded a new ad that claims Booker condones abortion at any stage of pregnancy and without restrictions. "He supports late-term and partial-birth abortion and opposes safety regulations," the ad states.

We checked with the Booker campaign. "We can all agree that we want to prevent unintended pregnancies, and therefore the need for abortion," a spokesman said. "Mayor Booker supports Roe v. Wade, which allows women the right to choose up to the point of viability."

As for late-term and partial-birth abortions? "Cory Booker does not oppose restrictions on post-viability abortions if exceptions are made for the health and the life of the mother," the spokesman said.

Source: Politifact.com FactCheck on New Jersey Senate race, Sept. 1, 2013

BROKEN PROMISE: *Booker attempted to appear more moderate on abortion by parsing meaningless differences in policy: we call that "legalism." We think Booker took the easy way out by lying to avoid controversy during the campaign, and then showed his true colors later in the Senate.*

ANALYSIS: *Booker was pressed for specifics during the campaign and said he accepted "post-viability exceptions." But then he co-sponsored a bill that banned post-viability exceptions. Booker might say, "Well, SOME post-viability exceptions are ok, but not THOSE post-viability exceptions." But THOSE post-viability exceptions are the currently controversial ones, which come up on pro-life bills for votes in the Senate.*

Actions Taken on Abortion

Ban anti-abortion limitations on abortion services

Booker co-sponsored the Women's Health Protection Act; *Congressional summary*: makes the following limitations concerning abortion services unlawful & prohibits their imposition by any government:

- a requirement that a medical professional perform specific tests, unless generally required in the case of medically comparable procedures;

- a limitation on an abortion provider's ability to delegate tasks;

- a limitation on an abortion provider's ability to prescribe or dispense drugs based on her or his good-faith medical judgment;

- a requirement or limitation concerning the physical plant, equipment, staffing, or hospital transfer arrangements;

- a requirement that, prior to obtaining an abortion, a woman make medically unnecessary visits to the provider of abortion services or to any individual or entity that does not provide such services;

- a prohibition or ban prior to fetal viability

Opponent's argument against (Live Action News): This is Roe v. Wade on steroids. The sponsors of this pro-abortion bill seem to feel that pro-life bills have had their time in this country, and that we must now turn back to abortion. The bill also demonstrates that its proponents have likely not even bothered attempting to understand the laws they are seeking to undo, considering that such laws are in place to regulate abortion in order to make it safer. Those who feel that abortion is best left up for the states to decide will also find this bill problematic with its overreach. Sadly, the bill also uses the Fourteenth Amendment to justify abortion, as the Supreme Court did, even though in actuality it would make much more sense to protect the lives of unborn Americans.

Source: H.R.3471 & S.1696 on Nov. 13, 2013

Campaign Promises on Family Planning

Vigorously defend access to affordable birth control

While we have made gains in Washington, there is more that needs to be done. As your Senator, I will not rest until every New Jerseyan has access to affordable, high-quality health care. My priorities will include:

- Working to have our nation better invest in prenatal and early childhood health initiatives – proven measures that elevate lifelong health and reduce long-term burden on taxpayers;

- Helping our nation develop strategies for wellness and preventative health. This is truly the best way to reduce health care cost and elevate the quality of life;

- Vigorously defending women's access to health care, affordable birth control, and protecting every woman's right to make decisions about her reproductive health.

Source: CoryBooker.com Senate campaign website, Nov. 3, 2013

KEPT PROMISE: *Booker promoted family planning as a health issue as well as a social justice issue during the campaign; and defended it under the same terms while in the Senate.*

ANALYSIS: *Family planning needed defending in the Senate because, unlike Booker, Senate Republicans carefully distinguish between abortion and birth control or other forms of family planning. The letter on the opposite page is, on its surface, about federal funding for all aspects of family planning, but really it's about federal funding for Planned Parenthood abortion clinics. Planned Parenthood separates their family planning funds (which are federally-provided under Title X) from their abortion funds (which are not federally-provided at all). But Republicans recognize that shutting down the federal funding to the non-abortion parts of Planned Parenthood will also shut down the abortion parts. In a sense, Booker pretends that the two parts can be separated – but he made the same pretense during the campaign as he makes while in the Senate, so he kept his promise.*

Actions Taken on Family Planning

Keep federal funding for family planning clinics

We write today with great concern regarding Republican efforts to undermine care at our nation's family planning clinics. For women in every U.S. state and especially in rural and struggling communities, Title X health centers are a vital resource for preventive and primary care. The recent vote in the House to overturn rules protecting Title X health centers would deny women access to this care and permit discrimination against providers. We urge you to protect the health and wellbeing of millions of women by committing not to bring this harmful legislation to the Senate floor.

The Title X family planning provider network is the only federal grant program dedicated solely to providing individuals with comprehensive family planning and related preventive health services. In 2015, Title X provided basic primary and preventive health care services such as pap tests, breast exams, and HIV testing to more than four million low-income women and men at over 4,000 health centers. In large part due to this work, the U.S. unintended pregnancy rate is at a 30-year low, and rates of teenage pregnancy are the lowest in our nation's history. The success of the program is dependent on funding that is awarded and available to the most qualified health care providers. Without this assurance, family planning providers lose access to federal family planning resources and in turn have fewer resources to see patients, resulting in less access to care.

Family planning services, like those provided at Planned Parenthood and other family planning centers, should be available to all women, no matter where they live or how much money they make. It is critical that you take a stand and protect women's health against efforts to undermine reproductive health care and roll back women's health advances.

Source: Letter to the Senate Majority Leader Mitch McConnell from 46 senators, March 1, 2017

Campaign Promises on Family Leave

Society struggles without paid family leave

Our society claims to value children, but struggling mothers get no paid family leave. The U.S. is the only developed country that doesn't offer government- sponsored paid family leave. Almost all of the world's nations — from Afghanistan to the Democratic Republic of the Congo — offer this kind of support, but we don't.

Where people have no paid family leave, or vacation days, a child's illness is so much more than the minor stress and inconvenience my mother endured when I got sick. There is the added stress of how to pay a doctor or a co-pay, how to make rent if you miss a day's work to stay home with your child, how to cope with not being there when your son, hospitalized for asthma, calls for his mother.

Source: United, by Senator Cory Booker, p.133-4, Feb. 16, 2016

KEPT PROMISE: *Booker promoted paid family leave during the campaign; and co-sponsored legislation to advance it, while in the Senate.*

ANALYSIS: *This is the active area of "family policy" that garners bipartisan support: not the anti-gay "family values" of the conservative right, and not the pro-choice "family planning" of the liberal left. Ivanka Trump famously persuaded Donald Trump to support THIS sort of family values during the presidential campaign – so now senators on both sides of the aisle are attempting to steer this topic into signable legislation.*

Actions Taken on Family Leave

Job-protected time off for bereavement and illness

Booker announced that he has signed on to a legislative effort that would expand the Family and Medical Leave Act to protect grieving parents from losing their jobs in the event of a child's death.

The Parental Bereavement Act would amend the Family Medical Leave Act (FMLA) to give parents up to 12 weeks of unpaid, but job-protected, time off of work to cope with the death of a child. Roughly 3,000 American children between the ages of one and 14 die suddenly each year from accidents.

"Parents grieving the loss of a child shouldn't have to fear losing their job too," Booker said. "This bill is a common sense expansion of family protections that Americans rely on."

Booker also supports legislation that would provide paid family leave for Americans. Booker is an original cosponsor of the Healthy Families Act, which would allow workers to earn up to seven paid sick days per year to recover from illness or take care of a loved one. He also is a cosponsor of the Family and Medical Insurance Leave Act, which would establish a federal paid family leave policy.

"Paid family leave provides stability for families. Unfortunately, American family leave laws lag behind the rest of the world and we have a long way to go to catch up," Booker said. "Congress must act to strengthen these laws."

Source: Press Release from Senate office booker.senate.gov,
February 5, 2016

Campaign Promises on Same-Sex Marriage

Supports gay marriage: We are all equal under the law

[Booker's opponent Steve] Lonegan said "marriage is the greatest institution made by man" because "it's about the children." Asked whether he believes gay couples should have children, he quipped: "That would be a biological phenomenon." He then added: "I have mixed feelings about that."

A state Superior Court judge last week ruled New Jersey must allow gay couples to get married. Lonegan said the ruling on same-sex marriage should be made by the state Legislature or people of New Jersey, not a judge. Booker disagreed and said that as an African American, he would "not be standing here right now if judges didn't say everyone in America is equal under the law." He added, "The ability to marry the person you love is one of the most fundamental liberties in America."

Source: Newark Star-Ledger coverage of N.J. Senate debate, Oct. 5, 2013

Equal marriage rights for same-sex couples are coming

I don't think that we as a country should allow religious differences to undermine the forces that protect the individuality and the uniqueness and diversity of our nation. I think one of the most intimate choices one can make is who to spend your life with and to be able to choose someone to be your life partner, and proclaim it to the world, "This is my spouse. This is my chosen soul that I am going to take on the world with." To me this is such an intimate personal issue, but it also should be a fundamental right when you are in America. I think it's wrong that I can marry certain Americans or Newark residents and I can't marry others. This is a same sex couple. Right now, the law says in New Jersey that I can't marry them. Until I can marry people equally, I don't think I should be doing that at all. I think people need to know what I know with great certainty that equal marriage rights are coming.

Source: Cory Booker column on Huffington Post, Nov. 4, 2008

Actions Taken on Same-Sex Marriage

Officiated same-sex marriage at first moment allowed

In what he called one of the "deepest honors of my life," Newark Mayor and New Jersey Senator-elect Cory Booker officiated the weddings of nine gay, lesbian, and straight couples in City Hall shortly after midnight. Booker announced to the crowd, "All right, ladies and gentleman, it is officially past midnight. Marriage is equal in New Jersey." Booker's office organized the 12:01 a.m. ceremony after a trial-court judge ruled that same-sex couples could begin marrying in NJ on Oct. 21.

When Booker reached the line in his script that prompts attendees for objections — to "speak now or forever hold your peace" — a man broke the silence. "It is unlawful in the eyes of God," he yelled, carrying a sign with bible script written on it. After the heckler had been removed from the room, Booker said, "Not hearing any substantive and worthy objections, I now will proceed with the vows."

For seven years as mayor of Newark, Booker has turned down requests to officiate weddings as a way of "protesting the painful reality that I could not marry all citizens equally," he said after the proceedings. "So I made a decision when I became mayor that, for the last seven and a half years, that I wasn't going to marry anybody until I could marry everybody."

Source: Buzzfeed.com, "Booker Shuts Down Heckler," Oct. 21, 2013

BACKGROUND: *As of the 2012 election, 13 states allowed some sort of same-sex civil unions, while 29 states had laws defining marriage as one-man-one-woman. In late 2014, the Supreme Court ruled that same-sex marriage was a guaranteed right, which legalized same-sex marriage in all 50 states.*

KEPT PROMISE: *Booker took a strong stance on marriage equality long before many politicians "evolved" to supporting gay marriage.*

ANALYSIS: *Hillary Clinton, for example, "evolved" from opposing gay marriage in the 1990s to support by 2016, which she claims coincided with America's "evolution" on the subject. Booker's "evolution" occurred long before he entered politics (see next page).*

Campaign Promises on LGBT Rights

Growing up gay today is like growing up black in past

I was in my tolerance stage or the "I don't give a damn if someone is gay, just as long as they don't bother me" stage. I was well trained in my tolerance. I stopped telling my gay jokes. Of course, I had my gay friend.

Yet, while I was highly adroit at maintaining an air of acceptance, I couldn't betray my feelings. I was disgusted by gays. The thought of two men kissing each other was about as appealing as a frontal lobotomy. Allow me to be more direct, escaping the euphemisms of my past – I hated gays. The disgust and latent hostility I felt toward gays were subcategories of hatred, plain and simple. Thoughts would flash in my mind, "What sinners I am amongst" or "How unnatural these people are."

It takes too much energy to hate. Our gay counselor showed me that, when I was a freshman. A beautiful man whose eloquent and poignant truths began to move me past tolerance.

He told me of the years of denial and the pain of always feeling different. And he told me of the violence. It was chilling to find that so much of the testimony he shared with me was almost identical to stories my grandparents told me about growing up black. People found it revolting to share a meal with them and often felt it to be their duty to beat them so that they would learn proper living.

Well, it didn't take me long to realize that the root of my hatred did not lie with gays but with myself. It was my problem. A problem I dealt with by ceasing to tolerate gays and instead seeking to embrace them. In these efforts I have found another community with which I feel akin and from which I draw strength. The gay people with whom I am close are some of the strongest, most passionate and caring people I know and their demands for justice are no less imperative than those of any other community.

Source: Stanford Daily column (student newspaper), vol. 201, #33, April 8, 1992

Actions Taken on LGBT Rights

Voted YES on Employment Non-Discrimination Act

- Prohibits an employer from discriminating against, failing to hire, refusing to hire, or discharging any individual on the basis of the individual's actual or perceived "sexual orientation" or "gender identity." Applies same rules to membership in labor organizations.

- Defines "gender identity" as the gender-related identity, appearance, or mannerisms or other gender-related characteristics of an individual, with or without regard to the individual's designated sex at birth.

- Authorizes the Equal Employment Opportunity Commission to administer and enforce the provisions of this bill in the same manner as title VII of the Civil Rights Act of 1964 and the Government Employee Rights Act of 1991.

- Exempts corporations, associations, educational institutions, institutions of learning, and societies that are exempt from the religious discrimination provisions of title VII of the Civil Rights Act of 1964 from the provisions of this bill.

Source: S 815, ENDA, introduced April 25, 2013;
passed Senate Nov. 7, 2013

KEPT PROMISE: *Booker promised to push for gay civil rights, and he has done so with ENDA and other legislation.*

ANALYSIS: *Booker views gay rights as a civil rights matter: that is the defining difference between the progressive stance and the liberal stance. Liberals say that gay marriage should be allowed now because the majority of Americans support it; that implies that states could vote against same-sex marriage by majority opinion. Progressive support of gay marriage as a civil right means that judges can overrule the majority opinion, like judges overruled the majority to protect minority rights in the 1960s. The ENDA bill above is therefore progressive legislation: it asserts that enforcement of gay rights will be treated the same as minority rights in the 1960s.*

Campaign Promises on Religious Freedom

Show your religion in how you treat other people

Before you speak to me about your religion, first show it to me in how you treat other people; before you tell me how much you love your God, show me in how much you love all His children; before you preach to me of your passion for your faith, teach me about it through your compassion for your neighbors. In the end, I'm not as interested in what you have to tell or sell as in how you choose to live and give.

Source: Facebook posting, facebook.com/corybooker, April 24, 2012

Even those with no religion are entitled to rights

Our nation was not founded because we all looked alike, or prayed alike, or descended from the same family tree. But our founders, in this, the oldest constitutional democracy, put forth on this earth the idea that all are created equal; that we all have inalienable rights.

And upon this faithful foundation we built a great nation, and today, no matter who you are — rich or poor, Asian or white, man or woman, gay or straight, any religion or none at all — you are entitled to the full rights and responsibilities of citizenship.

Our founders put forth a Declaration of Independence, but also made a historic declaration of interdependence. They knew that if this country was to survive, we had to make an unusual and extraordinary commitment to one another.

Source: Democratic National Convention speech, July 26, 2016

BROKEN PROMISE: *Booker's campaign statement appeared to be moderate on religion – perhaps even making him a member of the "religious left." But his actions in the Senate have been hard-core in favor of separating church and state. We'll call that "**evolution**."*

ANALYSIS: *The term "religious freedom" has a very different meaning depending on party. For Republicans, it means the right to apply your religious beliefs on your employees or customers – which in the Hobby Lobby case, meant they could decline abortion coverage. For Democrats, "religious freedom" instead means the government has no business getting involved in approving or disapproving of religions.*

Actions Taken on Religious Freedom

Fix Hobby Lobby: it's not about religious freedom

Booker urged Congress today to pass a law to fight the U.S. Supreme Court's controversial ruling allowing some religious-leaning companies to refuse paying for insurance coverage for contraception under ObamaCare. Booker vowed to work with fellow Democrats in Congress to draft legislation that would "fix" the ruling.

The nation's highest court voted 5-4 that companies with religious objections can dodge the requirement to pay for insurance coverage for contraception under ObamaCare, saying it violates a federal law protecting religious freedom. The ruling favored art-&-crafts chain Hobby Lobby, among about 50 companies to sue over the ObamaCare requirement.

Source: Newark Star-Ledger, "Hobby Lobby ruling," July 1, 2014

Religious freedom means no religious registry

[Booker] introduced legislation that would block a registry of people based on their religion. "Religious freedom and freedom from discrimination are fundamental rights central to the very idea of being an American," Sen. Booker said. "Forcing people to sign up for a registry based on their religion, race, or national origin does nothing to keep America secure. It does, however, undermine the freedom of religion guaranteed by our Constitution and promote the false notion that people of certain faiths and nationalities are inherently suspect. Our legislation would block Donald Trump and subsequent administrations from infringing on religious liberty by creating an immigration-related religious registry. Throughout our history, the US has been a beacon of hope for those seeking religious freedom. We must ensure this legacy lasts forever into the future."

Trump has repeatedly promised to establish a registry of individuals based on their religion. National origin-based immigration registry systems have proven ineffective at combatting terrorism. The George W. Bush-era National Security Entry-Exit Registration System registered over 83,000 individuals from 24 Muslim-majority countries, but yielded zero terrorism convictions.

Source: Press Release on Protect American Families Act, Jan. 5, 2017

Campaign Promises on Affirmative Action

Creative civil rights activism revealed rampant injustice

Decades before, through creative acts of protest, courageous civil rights activists had revealed to the public at large the injustices that were rampant throughout our society. The resulting outrage fomented action that created change.

Our housing policy in this country, from the local level to the federal level, was exactly what the civil rights movement was fighting against: segregation, discrimination, the erecting of walls between people. We designed housing policy so as to obscure our ability to see each other, to prevent ourselves from having to connect with others and confront the truth about what they were enduring. We allowed injustice to grow strong and persist in a way that is utterly contrary to our country's core values, that insults our best conceptions of humanity.

Source: United, by Senator Cory Booker, p.103-4, Feb. 16, 2016

MLK's dream still demands work to do, after 50 years

Q: Here's what you said at the Martin Luther King ceremony:

(VIDEO) BOOKER: The truth of the matter is that the dream still demands that the moral conscience of our country still calls us, that hope still needs heroes. We need to understand that there is still work to do.

Q: What is the legacy of the "I Have a Dream" speech? There's only one other African American U.S. senator; one African American governor; one African American president. Progress, but still uneven when it comes to elected office. Is that how Dr. King saw the dream playing out 50 years later?

BOOKER: Well, I think that these positions are important. But I think the matter in what drove the March [on Washington], was not simply propelling people to elected office, it was dealing with the larger issues of inequality. Not only racial inequality, but frankly the challenge we faced then in our nation till now and the dramatic differences between rich and poor and the challenges we have and had then in America and we still have now with poverty.

Source: Meet the Press on New Jersey Senate race, Aug. 25, 2013

Actions Taken on Affirmative Action

Fund minority businesses with KIVA microloans

We brought KIVA into Newark, which is a technological platform [for crowdsourcing microloans]. Small businesses would not need to get loans from banks anymore. We started off with a Latina businesswoman who could not get a $5,000 loan from a traditional bank because she didn't seem credit-worthy. But through an online platform, people like you and I can help to expand businesses in our city. And by the way, their repayment rates are as good or better than people that think banks are great. These are the things we can expand. But it actually has federal implications as well. How can we better start small businesses around our country? How can we go in creative ways to get access to capital in this bad economy?

So, from technology innovations to innovations around everything from education to health care, things we have done in Newark, I hope to help inform federal policy. But from day one, I want to be helping folks around New Jersey in very pragmatic ways to get the support they need to start a business, to go to college, to make their neighborhood safer.

Source: Interview on MSNBC's Rachel Maddow Show, Oct. 22, 2013

KEPT PROMISE: *Booker's campaign rhetoric showed that he was well-versed in the theory of affirmative action; his actions show that he puts that theory in practice.*

ANALYSIS: *Many affirmative action advocates stop at the stage of rhetorical theory. Most push for state hiring with race and gender quotas – that sort of program is limited to the public sector and only provides a "model" for the private sector, and hence has no only a limited effect on changing society. The Kiva program addresses an important aspect of gender and racial discrimination in the private sector: it bypasses banks that historically have discriminated against women and minorities. The Kiva program also fits Booker's preferred model of private-public partnerships.*

Campaign Promises on Pay Equity for Women

Gender wage gap problematic; minority wage gap worse

America has come a long way in the struggle for equal rights … but we are still far short of realizing the promise of our ideals. For every dollar a New Jersey man earns, on average, a woman earns only 79¢ for equal work. That reflects some improvement from the 59¢ women made 50 years ago, but the wage gap today is even more problematic because the number of female breadwinners has quadrupled. To add to this injustice, nationally, African American and Latina women earn only 64¢ and 55¢, respectively, for every dollar their male counterparts earn.

Our work will not be done until we live in a nation where equal work means equal pay, where a woman and her doctor make her health care decisions, and where access to quality preventative care is the priority it should be. And that's why, as your Senator, I will work to make the long overdue promises advanced by the 2009 enactment of the Lilly Ledbetter Fair Pay Act a reality by supporting further efforts to close the income gap between men and women, including the Paycheck Fairness Act and raising the federal minimum wage.

As your Senator, I will make sure that the government contract procurement process promotes women-owned businesses and female entrepreneurs, as well as fair pay.

I will follow the lead of the many courageous women who have helped achieve the progress we have made, and will do all I can to support their efforts to build a country in which gender does not impact how much you bring home in your paycheck, to what extent you control decisions about your health, or how far you're likely to go in your career.

Source: CoryBooker.com Senate campaign website, Nov. 3, 2013

KEPT PROMISE: *Booker made very specific promises on pay equity for women, and he converted those promises into bill sponsorships.*

ANALYSIS: *The gender pay gap is the focal point of affirmative action legislation for the Democratic Party. Booker's co-sponsored legislation on the opposite page is "cutting edge" but not very cutting – it addresses only women, and not minorities. Booker addresses the "minority wage gap" above but it's not yet in legislation.*

Actions Taken on Pay Equity for Women

Enforce against wage discrimination based on gender

Booker co-sponsored the Paycheck Fairness Act; in which Congress finds the following:

- Women have entered the workforce in record numbers over the past 50 years.

- Despite the enactment of the Equal Pay Act in 1963, many women continue to earn significantly lower pay than men for equal work. The pay disparities can only be due to continued intentional discrimination or the lingering effects of past discrimination.

- The existence of such pay disparities depresses the wages of working families who rely on the wages of all members of the family; and undermines women's retirement security.

- Artificial barriers to the elimination of discrimination in the payment of wages on the basis of sex continue to exist decades after the enactment of the Fair Labor Standards Act of 1938.

- The Department of Labor and the Equal Employment Opportunity Commission have important and unique responsibilities to help ensure that women receive equal pay for equal work.

- The Department of Labor is responsible for investigating and prosecuting equal pay violations, especially systemic violations, and in enforcing all of its mandates.

- The Equal Employment Opportunity Commission is the primary enforcement agency for claims made under the Equal Pay Act.

- With a stronger commitment [to enforcement], increased information on wage data and more effective remedies, women will be better able to recognize and enforce their rights.

- Certain employers have already made great strides in eradicating unfair pay disparities in the workplace and their achievements should be recognized.

Source: S.84 and H.R.377 introduced on Jan. 23, 2013

Campaign Promises on College Policy

Ensure that college tuition is not a long-term burden

We must do more to make college more affordable for anyone who is seeking to advance their education. Ensuring more ready access to college is not only about providing all Americans with an opportunity to succeed based on their merits, but is also an investment in our economy.

That's why, as mayor, I established a program at Newark's Financial Empowerment Center that reached more than one thousand college-bound Newarkers through financial aid workshops. It has helped Newark students receive approximately $1.3 million in Pell Grant awards.

The very fact that Congress has been paralyzed in the face of student loan rates that are set to double is only the latest piece of evidence that we are not putting education first. The situation is absolutely unacceptable: Tuition rates are climbing and student loan debt has topped over a trillion dollars nationally. More than 100,000 low-income students are denied the ability to go to college every year, and a typical low-income family dedicates the equivalent of more than 70 percent of its annual income to send a child to college for a year. Here in New Jersey, as in many states, there has been a massive spike in college enrollment paired with steep cuts in state support, putting tremendous pressure on tuition.

As your senator, I will support access to the education our kids need to succeed by doing all I can to ensure paying for that education is not a barrier or long-term burden.

Source: CoryBooker.com Senate campaign website, Nov. 3, 2013

KEPT PROMISE: *Booker's campaign called for extending government assistance to the first two years of college; his bill on the opposite page called for two years of college tuition free.*

ANALYSIS: *Booker agrees with the mainstream Democratic Party on reducing college costs – but his agreement on higher education does not extend down to grade school. We explore Booker's disagreement with Democrats in the following pages.*

Actions Taken on College Policy

Make two years of community college free

Booker introduced the America's College Promise Act: Nearly a century ago, a movement made high school widely available, which helped lead to rapid growth in the education and skills training of Americans, driving decades of economic growth and prosperity. President Obama asked Congress to make another bold investment in our nation's students by making two years of community college free. The America's College Promise Act does exactly that:

- Creates a new partnership between the federal government and states to help them waive resident tuition in two years of community and technical college programs for eligible students;

- Provides a federal match of $3 for every $1 invested by the state to waive community college tuition and fees for eligible students before other financial aid is applied;

- Ensures that programs offer academic credits which are fully transferable to four-year institutions in their state, or occupational training that leads to industry credentials;

- Maintains and encourages state funding for higher education; and

- Establishes a new grant program to provide pathways to success at minority serving institutions by helping them cover a significant portion of tuition and fees for the first two years of attendance for low-income students.

Community, technical, and tribal colleges enroll forty percent of all college students today, and offer students lower tuition, open admission policies, and convenient locations. They also offer academic programs and an affordable route to a four-year college degree. Community colleges are uniquely positioned to partner with employers to create tailored training programs to meet economic needs within their communities such as nursing, health information technology, and advanced manufacturing.

Source: Press release from Tammy Baldwin, Senate sponsor of
S.1716 & H.R.2962, introduced July 8, 2015

Campaign Promises on Race to the Top

Fundamental right to high quality public education

I believe that access to a high quality public education is a fundamental American right and that fully realizing the genius of our children is vital to the health of our economy and a strong and secure future for our country. Knowing this, I pulled together stakeholders to develop strategies and take action for our kids. I then raised over $200 million to launch initiatives that would help our public schools meet their enormous obligations. We have a lot to be proud of in Newark, including:

- *More kids in preschool:* 61 percent more 3 and 4 year olds enrolled in public preschool;

- *Tackling illiteracy:* Raised philanthropy to provide 120,000 books for nearly 12,000 low-income students at 20 Newark public schools to help build home libraries;

- *Options:* Attracted new public school models, leading to families having more quality public education choices;

- *Empowering teachers:* Establish a "Teacher Innovation Fund" that pays for ideas teachers have to improve student outcomes;

- *Rewarding good teachers:* Facilitated a groundbreaking teacher's union contract that made the district the first in New Jersey to offer performance bonuses to effective teachers, and holding accountable ineffective teachers who are failing our kids.

Source: CoryBooker.com Senate campaign website, Nov. 3, 2013

BROKEN PROMISE: *Booker is **muddying the water** here — basically Booker was afraid to say what he REALLY believed in – because he knew that the mainstream Democratic Party would strongly disagree.*

ANALYSIS: *Booker's rhetoric misuses standard liberal pro-public school phrases. "Empowering teachers" to liberals means "empowering teachers' unions" – exactly the opposite of what Booker did. His subtly-worded "options" line did include "new models" – charter schools and, later, vouchers. This is the education policy equivalent of a pro-choice advocate saying "I'm pro-life for the mother" – which everyone would recognize as misleading.*

Actions Taken on Race to the Top

Supports "Race to the Top" education reform

Booker's major substantive difference with many progressives is on education policy. He is — like President Obama — an advocate of the "education reform" movement; he has backed New Jersey Governor Chris Christie's expansion of charter schools and merit pay for teachers, as well as a form of vouchers for some impoverished areas. He sits on the board of Democrats for Education Reform. The school-reform issue is the subject of a major schism in today's Democratic Party; Obama's "Race to the Top" education initiative, which has encouraged state-level reforms, has infuriated traditional Democratic allies but also drawn support from many party officeholders.

Source: The Atlantic, "Why Do Liberals Hate Booker," Aug. 23, 2013

Star fundraiser for Democrats for Education Reform

Booker's 2002 campaign inspired hedge-fund managers to seek out and support more Democrats who embraced charter schools and opposed the influence of teachers' unions on the party. They ultimately formed a political action committee, Democrats for Education Reform, with Booker as one of their star fundraisers. The group's beneficiaries would come to include the 2004 Senate candidate, Barack Obama.

These "venture philanthropists" called themselves investors rather than donors, seeking returns in the form of sweeping changes to public schooling. President Obama incorporated many of these goals into *Race to the Top*, a $4.3 billion initiative that induced states to expand charter schools and to tie teachers' evaluations, pay, and job security to growth in their students' standardized test scores. The stated goal was to put single-minded focus on what was best for children, even at the expense of upending adult lives and livelihoods.

In the beginning, Democratic politicians almost universally spurned the cause, as did many African American leaders, perceiving these efforts as threats to the Democratic base in cities: unions, public sector jobs, and politicians who doled them out.

Source: The Prize: Who's in Charge of America's Schools? by Dale Russakoff, pp. 9, 13, Sept. 8, 2015

Campaign Promises on Charter Schools

Charters & alternatives for persistently failing schools

In Newark, there are many models of success and we are aggressively working to replicate and expand them. Last year, Newark was selected as one of three cities for a huge investment in our charter schools. The goal is to make our entire charter school sector in Newark high quality in accordance with the highest and most uncompromising standards and outcomes and work to expand those schools so more Newark youth can have high quality choice.

We have recently begun a small school initiative for our high school students who are at risk of dropping out. Further, among other things, our new superintendent is looking to expand our magnet schools of excellence which have long waiting lists and completely reorganize our persistently failing schools.

Source: Cory Booker Blog, "A Hard Look at Education", May 11, 2009

BACKGROUND: *'Charter schools' are publicly-funded and publicly-controlled schools which are privately run. They are usually required to adhere to fewer district rules than regular public schools. The first charter schools started in Minnesota in 1991.*

By 2011, there were 5,600 public charter schools enrolling more than two million students nationwide. More than 400,000 students remain on wait lists to attend charter schools. Over 500 new public charter schools opened their doors in the 2011-12 school year, an estimated increase of 200,000 students. By the 2014-15 school year, the number of charter schools has increased to over 6,600.

Actions Taken on Charter Schools

Founded the Newark Charter School Fund

Q: I hear that the state is cutting back on school funding, and that the schools are laying off workers. Are our kids going to suffer?

A: The city and school budgets are separate, and the schools are under state control. The mayor and the council have no say over school personnel decisions. There is no question, though, that we should be concerned about the education afforded to Newark's children. The mayor has spent much of his energy and focus on improving the educational environment in the city. He has founded the Newark Charter School Fund, identified financial support for five new alternative schools, launched the Teacher Next project, create the YES Center, and runs the annual Mayor's Achievement Challenge.

Source: Introduced Budget: Mayor's Commentary Press Release, Feb 9, 2010

Brother runs a charter school in inner-city Memphis

Booker tells me about his admiration for his brother, Cary, who runs a charter school in inner-city Memphis. "My brother's done a great job of staying loyal to his truth," he says. "He's a much more humble guy than I am. He's just sort of a plodding, determined soul, trying to make a difference in as many people's lives as possible."

Source: Vogue magazine profile, "Local Hero Cory Booker," Dec. 19, 2012

KEPT PROMISE: *When talking about charter schools directly, Booker honestly supported them in his campaigns, and then supported them in office too.*

ANALYSIS: *Booker's reference to state control of the Newark school is because the Newark school district is one of three districts in New Jersey which came under state intervention due to the district failing to meet required corrective actions. The state intervention began in 1995, preceding Booker's time in city elected office, and provided Booker the opportunity for experimentation with charters and other methods.*

Campaign Promises on School Vouchers

Vouchers and charters can work in inner cities

I have always been, up until maybe four or five years ago, a strong advocate for the old-fashioned way of educating children. I supported public schools only. Even charter schools made me a little uncomfortable when I first heard about them. But after four or five years of working in inner city Newark, I began to rethink my situation, rethink my philosophy, rethink my views on public education, simply because of the realities I saw around me. Being outcome-focused started to change my view in favor of options like charter schools, contract schools and, yes, vouchers.

I challenge anybody to come into my city and walk with me and simply talk to these inner-city single mothers. You will see that they care more about the education of their children and are more informed than suburban soccer moms are in the towns where I grew up. They know what it is going to take to help their children achieve the American dream. They believe in [education and vouchers], and they still hold onto it.

Source: Manhattan Institute Civic Bulletin No. 25, "School Choice", Feb. 1, 2001

BACKGROUND: *'Vouchers' are a means of implementing school choice — parents are given a 'voucher' by the school district, which entitles them to, say, $4,000 applicable to either public school or private school tuition. The value of the voucher is generally lower than the cost of one year of public education (which averages $5,200), so private schools (where tuition averages $8,500) may require cash payment in addition to the voucher. Vouchers are controversial when they are used for parochial school tuition which critics claim amounts to state subsidy of religion in violation of the separation of church and state.*

Supports school voucher proposal, like other Democrats

U.S. Reps. Frank Pallone and Rush Holt took some shots at Booker, mostly for his support of a school voucher proposal offered by Gov. Chris Christie. "I very much disagree with Mayor Booker on this. I do not believe that vouchers are the answer," Pallone said. "I'm very concerned about how vouchers, which he supports, will take away funding from public schools. I believe in public schools."

When Booker responded that he, too, believes in public schools and that he helped bring $100 million in philanthropic funds into the city's school system, Booker said both Pallone and Holt had voted in favor of the Washington DC Opportunity Scholarship Program — a voucher-like program that gives scholarships to low-income children. "While they're criticizing me I'd like them both to explain why they voted for the same position I have," Booker said. The vote Booker referenced was actually a much larger appropriations bill that included the program.

Source: Star-Ledger coverage of N.J. Senate debate, Aug. 5, 2013

BROKEN PROMISE: *Booker **"muddies the water"** in his Senate debate, attempting to obfuscate his pro-voucher stance. Booker felt the need to muddy the water on this issue because most Democrats disagree with Booker's pro-voucher stance. This is a defining difference between liberals and progressives: liberals (like Pallone and Holt) oppose vouchers in solidarity with public school teacher's unions; some progressives (like Booker) support vouchers because they are effective in inner cities. To be fully honest, Booker could have pointed out that yes, he supports vouchers, despite the Democratic Party and union stance against them.*

ANALYSIS: *Democrats generally do not support vouchers, and his two opponents certainly did not. Omnibus appropriations bills in Congress often includes line items with which members of Congress disagree – but they vote in favor of the overall legislative package because they agree with most of its content. For that reason, votes on omnibus bills are simply not meaningful as indicative of policy preferences. Booker pretends that his opponents' votes ARE meaningful.*

Chapter Four:
Cory Booker on International Issues

    * *indicates broken promise*

  * indicates broken promise

Campaign Promises on Domestic Spying

Public oversight needed for NSA domestic spying

Both Booker and [opponent Bogota Mayor Steve] Lonegan, on their campaign websites, offer their views on a range of foreign policy issues. Booker calls for boosting cyber security, asserting that NJ's power plants, oil pipelines and water systems remain vulnerable to a terrorist attack. Lonegan supports ending the surveillance of US citizens via the National Security Agency, which he has made a central campaign issue.

Booker has been less vocal on that topic, but says on his website that "we failed as a nation to thoroughly debate and create public oversight before this highly-questionable data collection began."

Lonegan opposes any United Nations treaties that would undercut U.S. sovereignty. Booker casts environmentalism in a national security context in endorsing further development of clean energy sources. He asserts that the U.S. is sending billions of dollars overseas to obtain oil, which ends up aiding terrorist groups and hostile regimes.

Source: WHYY NewsWorks.org on N.J. Senate race, Oct. 14, 2013

Founding principle: make laws open to public debate

I was deeply troubled by recent revelations of the scope of the National Security Agency's domestic data collection. We failed as a nation to thoroughly debate and create public oversight before this highly questionable data collection began. It is time to bring this program to light and fix that error.

It is a basic principle of our founding that laws be open to public debate and inspection. We must update the rules that permitted this program to exist and ensure Congress, the courts, and the people have access and oversight. We need to vigorously guard our 4th Amendment privacy protections while still protecting Americans from terrorism. There are serious questions about whether this program successfully does that, and we cannot ask these questions after the fact again.

Source: CoryBooker.com Senate campaign website, Nov. 3, 2013

Actions Taken on Domestic Spying

USA FREEDOM Act:
Restrict domestic monitoring of phone calls

Booker co-sponsored the Uniting and Strengthening America by Fulfilling Rights and Ensuring Effective Discipline Over Monitoring Act of 2014 or the USA FREEDOM Act: *Congressional Summary:*

- Requires the FBI, in applications seeking phone call detail records, to include a statement of facts showing: (1) reasonable grounds to believe that the call detail records are relevant; and (2) a reasonable, articulable suspicion that the specific selection term is associated with a foreign power engaged in international terrorism.

- Requires a judge approving the release, on a daily basis, of call detail records; and to limit production to a period of 180 days.

- Requires FISA court orders approving the production of tangible things to include each specific selection term used as the basis for such production.

- Amends the USA PATRIOT Act to audit the effectiveness and use of FISA authority to obtain production of information or tangible things, including an examination of whether procedures adequately protect the constitutional rights of U.S. persons.

- Requires the Director of National Intelligence to conduct a declassification review of each decision, order, or opinion issued by the FISA court; and make such decisions, orders, or opinions publicly available to the greatest extent practicable, subject to permissible redactions.

Source: USA FREEDOM Act, S.2685, introduced July 29, 2014

KEPT PROMISE: Booker's campaign opposed domestic spying; his actions in the Senate deliver on that promise.

ANALYSIS: Booker connected openness with domestic spying during his campaign; the legislation above translates that as "declassification." Openness or "transparency" is a core progressive value. Without transparency in government, in the immortal words of Donald Rumsfeld, "There are things we don't know we don't know."

Campaign Promises on Cybersecurity

Protect critical infrastructure from cyberattack

America's critical infrastructure – our power plants, oil pipelines, and water systems – are at serious risk of cyber attack. The vast majority of this critical infrastructure is privately owned. Yet today, if a major cyber attack took place on a telecom company or financial institution, that company wouldn't even know who to call to report it. New Jersey, with its miles of pipeline, dense petroleum storage, and many seaports – not to mention nuclear power plants – may be particularly vulnerable.

We need new ways to protect the computer-connected systems that keep lights on and banks open. Years ago we decided that physical security – fences and cameras — around sensitive sites like power plants was essential. Yet there is no requirement, or even voluntary standard, for putting virtual fences around the computers that run these facilities.

When critical infrastructure is attacked or essential data is stolen, companies need a clear way to report it to civilian authorities so that government has a picture of the threats and other companies can protect themselves from similar attacks. And because personal information like emails, phone calls, or medical records are easily caught up in the mix of technology, it's essential that privacy is protected.

Source: CoryBooker.com Senate campaign website, Nov. 3, 2013

KEPT PROMISE: *Booker promised to address cybersecurity in his campaign; and he did so in the Senate. Compare his "kept promises" on physical infrastructure on pp. 32-3.*

ANALYSIS: *Cybersecurity addresses international aspects of infrastructure, since cyberattacks can (and usually do) occur across international borders. The most well-known cyber-attack, "Stuxnet," was a secretly-produced US-Israeli computer worm that caused Iran's nuclear centrifuges to destroy themselves. Cyber-infrastructure policy suffers from the same problem as physical infrastructure: it is not glamorous, with rare exceptions like Stuxnet. If everything goes right with infrastructure, no one notices – which means there is little for politicians to show as results. For example, If Booker's National Guard plan is successful, he can say in five years, "We succeeded in nothing happening for the last five years" – important and accurate, but hardly a winning political statement!*

Actions Taken on Cybersecurity

Form National Guard Cyber Protection Team

U.S. Senators Gillibrand, Schumer, Menendez, and Booker announced their support for the New York and New Jersey Army National Guards' formation of a combined Cyber Protection Team. In a letter to the Army National Guard's Acting Director, the senators urged allowing the NY and NJ Army National Guards to form a joint team focused on addressing the growing cyber security threats. This new team would leverage their existing relationships with the Department of Homeland Security and their extensive training, to focus on combatting increasing cyber security threats to the region's critical infrastructure and networks.

"Technological innovations have greatly enhanced the lives of all Americans, however these advancements also bring unique cyber threats and challenges that we must collectively be prepared to face," said Senator Booker. "The New York and New Jersey National Guard have the expertise and knowledge to help tackle the serious regional cyber threats we face today. I'm pleased to support this important initiative that will help protect our critical infrastructure."

Currently, state Army National Guard units throughout the country are competing to form ten multi-state Cyber Protection Teams as part of the Army's efforts to build up its cyber capabilities. Senator Gillibrand introduced the Cyber Warrior Bill along with seven other senators in 2013, which called for the creation of a National Guard Cyber and Computer Network Incident Response Team in each state.

In their letter to the Army National Guard, the Senators wrote, "The NY-NJ Metropolitan Area has long been a primary target of our adversaries around the world. With the cyber world influencing many aspects of our economy and national security, we must be prepared to deter the growing threat to cyber networks in America's financial hub. Increasing resources and protection in the bi-state area not only decreases financial threat domestically, but also internationally."

Source: Press release on letter from 4 senators to Army National Guard,
November 17, 2014

Campaign Promises on Mideast Policy

Direct military intervention in Syria only as last resort

[All four Democratic Senate candidates] agreed the United States shouldn't take any rash actions against Russia for harboring Edward Snowden, but said it should pressure that country against instituting restrictive laws against gays. All four said the United States should be careful in how it deals with Syria, advocating against direct military intervention except as a last resort.

Source: Star-Ledger coverage of N.J. Senate debate, Aug. 5, 2013

We're spending billions on a war on unjust pretenses

My concern frankly is that we are putting billions of dollars on a war that we went into on unjust pretenses. And cities like mine who are struggling are actually getting a lot accomplished without the help of Federal programs that have dried up like the COPS program, putting more police officers on the street, like helping protect public housing authorities from crime.

Source: Bill Maher interview Democratic National Convention, Denver, Aug. 25, 2008

KEPT PROMISE: Booker questions the Iraq War and cautions against war with Syria in his campaign; he follows up on that promise with demands for Congressional approval for fighting ISIS and with calls for diplomacy over militarism.

ANALYSIS: Booker strikes a cautious tone on all issues related to Iraq and Syria, the two hotspots where future U.S. military intervention is most likely. His focus on the AUMF process hints that he would vote against a Congressional Authorization for the Use of Military Force. – if he voted for an AUMF in either Iraq or Syria we would rate that as a "broken promise" by muddying the waters on war process issues. Booker attempts to portray himself as a moderate on war issues – neither a bellicose hawk but not a peacenik dove – which portrayal is supported by his LACK of moderate caution on Iran on the following pages.

Actions Taken on Mideast Policy

ISIS is grave threat, but don't fight them without AUMF

I believe that ISIS poses a grave threat to innocent people and to our allies. Debate and authorization for operations against ISIS is long overdue, and authorizing operations and funding against ISIS in must-pass defense bill without an Authorization for the Use of Military Force (AUMF) is a disservice to our men and women in uniform and an abdication of Congress' responsibilities. That is why I co-sponsored an amendment to strike authorization for the training and equipping of the Syrian opposition until Congress passes an AUMF that permits such activities. While I am disappointed that our amendment was not included in the bill, I look forward to an opportunity for the full Senate to debate the parameters of our ongoing operations against ISIS.

*Source: Booker press release on Passage of National Defense
Authorization Act, February 2, 2015*

Trump denigrates relationships with Muslim countries

Q: How would Hillary Clinton's response to terrorism be different from that of President Obama?

BOOKER: Well, she is not running against President Obama. She is running against Donald Trump. And we know already what Donald Trump has said he was going to do, which is undermine key alliances like the NATO alliance which helps us to protect not only our country, but really fight against the war on terror. He wants to go against Muslims and denigrate relationships with Muslim countries, which include countries like Turkey. And already leaders there are worried about Trump. He wants to go back to doing things that are outrageous, like saying, "Hey, we're going to go after the families of terrorists; we're going to bring back torture." Donald Trump is dangerous and would make this world a far more dangerous place. In fact, he would undermine many of the things that are in place right now that would make us a much safer country.

*Source: CNN "State of the Union" interview during Democratic
Veepstakes, July 3, 2016*

Campaign Promises on Iranian Sanctions

All options on the table with Iran, including military

As a state sponsor of terrorism, Iran poses a threat to American security, a threat made worse by their pursuit of nuclear technology in defiance of the international community and their own treaty obligations. A nuclear-armed Iran is plainly unacceptable. It would pose serious threats to American interests and to our allies, particularly Israel.

Iranians recently elected a new president who has taken a less confrontational tone and positioned himself as open to negotiation. With the Supreme Leader of Iran holding control over final decisions regarding the nuclear program, it has yet to be seen if this openness is a delaying tactic to continue nuclear development or a genuine opportunity for engagement and negotiation.

The president is right to keep all options, including military action, on the table while vigorously pursuing both international sanctions and a negotiated settlement that prevents Iran from gaining nuclear weapons. Today, sanctions have imposed real and increasing harm on Iran's economy and isolated them from the international community. Pursuing these diplomatic and economic actions must continue while there is time, because while all options should remain on the table, the cost of military action to end the Iranian nuclear program could be very high for us and our allies in the region.

Source: CoryBooker.com Senate campaign website, Nov. 3, 2013

BACKGROUND: *President Obama announced the finalized nuclear deal with Iran in July 2015, after a seven-country negotiation (the United States, China, France, Germany, Iran, Russia, and the United Kingdom):*
- *Iran will reduce its stockpiles of enriched uranium.*
- *Iran will limit enrichment equipment and facilities.*
- *Iran will provide access for inspection about compliance.*
- *The UN, US, and EU will remove economic sanctions against Iran.*
- *Iran and the US exchanged prisoners (5 US citizens in Iran and 14 Iranians in the US imprisoned for violating the sanctions).*

Actions Taken on Iranian Sanctions

Iran must accept long-term intrusive nuke inspection

We all hope that nuclear negotiations succeed in preventing Iran from ever developing a nuclear weapons capability. For diplomacy to succeed, however, we must couple our willingness to negotiate with a united and unmistakable message to the Iranian regime. We write now to express our support for the following core principles and urge you to insist on their realization in a final agreement with Iran:

- Iran has no inherent right to enrichment under the Nuclear Non-Proliferation Treaty.

- Any agreement must dismantle Iran's nuclear weapons program and prevent it from ever having a path to a nuclear bomb.

- Iran has no reason to have an enrichment facility like Fordow, and that the regime must give up its heavy water reactor at Arak.

- Iran must submit to a long-term and intrusive inspection and verification regime.

- Finally, we believe Iran must not be allowed during these negotiations to circumvent sanctions.

Most importantly, Iran must clearly understand the consequences of failing to reach an acceptable final agreement. We must signal unequivocally to Iran that rejecting negotiations and continuing its nuclear weapon program will lead to much more dramatic sanctions, including further limitations on Iran's oil and petroleum exports.

Source: Letter to President Obama from 85 senators, March 18, 2014

KEPT PROMISE: *Booker took a tough line against Iran in his Senate campaign, and as a senator joined in calling for toughness against Iran in Obama's negotiations on the Iranian nuclear deal.*

ANALYSIS: *Booker wields the militaristic threat "all options on the table," which most progressives would label "saber-rattling at the bogeyman of the year." Evidently Booker believes in THIS bogeyman because he makes no such threats elsewhere in the Mideast (see pp. 110-1). Obama adhered to the Senate request, and Booker has expressed ongoing support of the negotiated Iran deal, unlike many Republicans.*

Campaign Promises on Israel/Palestine

Where Israel's security is at stake, so is America's

In an uncertain world, Israel continues to be an advocate for freedom, equality and democracy in the Middle East, protecting the rights of its citizens while upholding the values that Americans hold dear. From a strategic perspective, the US must continue to support Israel as a secure homeland for the Jewish people. Simply put, where Israel's security is at stake, America's security is at stake. We share strategic interests, face common threats and jointly aspire to achieve peace.

Ultimately, however, it is not only America's strategic self-interest, but also our shared respect for democratic values that anchors our special relationship with the Jewish state. American support for Israel has been at the center of our Mideast policy for six decades and must continue to be a central component of our foreign policy in the region.

Lasting security for Israel will ultimately require peace between Israel and its neighbors. That is why Americans must continue to work to facilitate direct negotiations that seek a two-state solution. However, it is the right of the Israeli government to make the tough decisions that are necessary to secure its future. The Palestinian people deserve a state, and one that allows them to prosper and thrive. That state, though, must not be a vehicle for the launching of attacks against Israel. During any eventual negotiation, certain things must remain non-negotiable, namely conditions that speak to Israel's right to exist as a secure Jewish state.

Source: CoryBooker.com Senate campaign website, Nov. 3, 2013

KEPT PROMISE: *Booker sounded like a hard-line pro-Israel supporter in his campaign, and followed up with hard-line pro-Israel legislation in the Senate (without any saber-rattling in either).*

ANALYSIS: *Supporting Israel is as safe a foreign policy stance as possible, which is why 79 senators (out of 100) co-sponsored the resolution on the opposite page, and only slightly fewer signed the pro-Israel letter below that. Progressives would accept much more conciliatory language on Palestinians; so we conclude that Booker is honestly pro-Israel (along with just about everyone else in the Senate).*

Actions Taken on Israel/Palestine

Two-state solution despite Israeli settlements on West Bank

Booker co-sponsored S.Res.6, which objects to U.N. Security Council Resolution 2334. Such resolution characterizes Israeli settlements in the West Bank as illegal and demands cessation of settlement activities.

- Calls for such resolution to be repealed or fundamentally altered and allows all final status issues toward a two-state solution to be resolved through direct bilateral negotiations.

- Granting membership to the Palestinians at international institutions outside of the context of a bilateral peace agreement with Israel would cause severe harm to the peace process.

- Urges the U.S. veto of all Security Council resolutions that recognize unilateral Palestinian actions or dictate terms and a time line for a solution to the Israeli-Palestinian conflict.

Source: Library of Congress summary of S.Res.6 & H.Res.11, Objecting to UN Resolution 2334, introduced on Jan. 3, 2017

Disallow Palestine from joining ICC to threaten Israel

We are deeply concerned by the decision of the Palestinian President Mahmoud Abbas to seek membership in the International Criminal Court (ICC), because the Palestinian Authority is not a state and its express intent is to use this process to threaten Israel.

Pres. Abbas' effort erodes the prospect for peace. Therefore, the U.S. must make clear that joining the ICC is not a legitimate or viable path for Palestinians. Israel is a major strategic partner of the U.S. and is facing increasing pressure from those who seek to delegitimize its very existence. Pres. Abbas' actions are intended to directly challenge Israel's legitimate right to defend its citizens and territories. The only realistic and sustainable path to resolving the Israeli-Palestinian conflict is through direct negotiations between Israel and the Palestinians.

Source: Letter to Secretary of State Kerry from 73 Senators, Jan. 29, 2015

Campaign Promises on Defense Spending

Maintain the strongest military force in the world

America has, and must continue to maintain, the strongest military force in the world. Our fighting men and women deserve the equipment they need to accomplish their missions, responsible planning necessary to ensure their success, and the care they were promised when they return home. These things are not negotiable.

The military threats of the future look very different than the challenges we faced in the 80s, 90s, or even just a few years ago, and America's military needs to keep up. Without a major adversary like the Soviet Union, smaller nontraditional conflicts and interventions are more likely to be the rule, even as we refocus on asserting power in the Pacific. That is why military spending should be driven by a strategy to meet future threats, rather than an arbitrary number invented for political posturing or an attempt to fight the wars of past.

For too long, Congress has been spending money on weapons our military doesn't want, weapons envisioned for wars never fought against enemies that no longer exist. That doesn't make us any safer – in fact, it makes us less safe by siphoning funds away from essential training and spending on relevant weapons systems. This irresponsible spending is even less acceptable at a time when sequestration is forcing across-the-board cuts – to military priorities essential and superfluous alike.

Source: CoryBooker.com Senate campaign website, Nov. 3, 2013

BACKGROUND: *The NDAA bill of 2015 including the usual panoply of billions in spending programs – presumably Booker would approve of some and disapprove of others. But this bill also included $89.2 billion in "Overseas Contingency Operations" for funding activities in war zones (like Afghanistan and Iraq). Obama vetoed the bill because he deemed that special funding dishonest, saying that it should be just another part of the regular defense budget. As part of the regular budget, it would be subject to "sequestration," and hence limited – whereas "emergency" war-zone spending in unlimited. Hence a NAY vote calls for limiting the defense budget by making all of it subject to sequestration.*

Actions Taken on Defense Spending

Respect sequestration on defense; no gimmicks

Booker voted NAY on HR 1735, which passed Senate 70-27 (Conference Report vote #277): The bill authorizes appropriations and sets forth policies regarding military construction for all military branches. This bill also authorizes appropriations for Overseas Contingency Operations (OCO), which are exempt from discretionary spending limits, in the amount of $89.2 billion. Other spending authorized:

- $89 billion   Overseas Contingency Operations
- $19 billion   Total Major Equipment Air Force
- $107 billion   Total Procurement
- $70 billion   Total Research, Development, Test & Evaluation
- $138 billion   Total Operation & Maintenance

Veto message from President Obama: While there are provisions in this bill that I support, this bill fails to authorize funding for our national defense in a fiscally responsible manner. It underfunds our military in the base budget, and instead relies on an irresponsible budget gimmick that has been criticized by members of both parties. Specifically, the bill's use of Overseas Contingency Operations funding—which was meant to fund wars and is not subject to budget caps—does not provide the stable, multi-year budget upon which sound defense planning depends. Because this bill authorizes base budget funding at sequestration levels, it threatens the readiness and capabilities of our military.

Source: HR 1735, National Defense Authorization Act, Oct. 7, 2015

BROKEN PROMISE: *Booker made conflicting promises for the "strongest military" and against "irresponsible spending," attempting to portray himself as a moderate on defense spending. He **contradicts himself** in that pair pf promises, and his promise on the "strongest military" was belied by his vote on Congress' biggest military package.*

ANALYSIS: *This is an "omnibus bill" with one overall vote on a very large spending package. It is normally very difficult to infer the meaning of an omnibus vote, but we infer that a NAY vote matches Obama's veto. Booker's ambiguous campaign promise has the usual purpose of attempting to please both sides at once by being intentionally vague.*

Campaign Promises on Veterans Issues

Incentives to train & hire troops returning home

For President Obama, "home of the brave" are not just the last words of our national anthem, but also a call to action. This is why the president's policies and our platform include incentives to train and hire our troops returning home. Not only because of our moral responsibility, but because it makes for a stronger, more secure American economy.

Source: Democratic National Convention speech, Sept. 4, 2012

KEPT PROMISE: *Booker promised during his campaign to do more for veterans, and in the Senate he has followed through.*

ANALYSIS: *This is the easiest promise a 2017 politician can make – and just about all politicians make this promise. It's easy to make the promise because 80% to 90% of Americans support more spending for veterans. And it's easy to keep the promise because spending a little more for veterans in each year's budget is what Congress excels at. Republicans like veteran spending because it shows support of the military in general; Democrats like veteran spending because they focus it on social programs like veterans' healthcare.*

The widespread support for spending on veterans was evidenced during President Trump's first address to a joint session of Congress – when Trump spoke about this issue, it was the only time that both sides of the aisle – both Democrats and Republicans – applauded.

The few Americans who oppose veteran spending – mostly hard-core progressives and libertarians – consider spending on veterans just a hidden way to increase the military budget. That applies to the entire Department of Veterans Affairs, as well as the Department of Homeland Security, and the half of the Department of Energy dedicated to nuclear weapons – they are not counted as part of the budget of the Department of Defense, but hard-core anti-military advocates think they should be.

Actions Taken on Veterans Issues

Exempt Veterans Affairs from federal hiring freeze

We are deeply troubled that your freeze on the hiring of federal civilian employees will have a negative and disproportionate impact on our nation's veterans. As such, we urge you to take stock of this hiring freeze's effect on our nation's veterans and exempt the Department of Veterans Affairs (VA) as well as any veterans seeking federal employment from your Memorandum Regarding the Hiring Freeze.

While there can be no debate that the federal government, including VA, should be more efficient in its delivery of services to all Americans, a hiring freeze at VA will delay veterans' access to health care and resolution of their disability claims, which for many of our nation's heroes provides a sole source of income to them and their families. Our nation's veterans should not be made to sacrifice any more than they already have while you review federal hiring.

- Have you considered how this hiring freeze will affect VA's ability to provide veterans with access to health care?

- Have you considered how this hiring freeze will affect VA's ability to provide veterans with decisions on their appeals for disability compensation?

- Have you considered how this hiring freeze will impact those veterans who apply to federal jobs?

Should you move forward with this hiring freeze, one issue that must not be overlooked is VA's little-known mission of providing support to national efforts to prepare for, respond to, and recover from natural disasters, acts of terrorism, and man-made catastrophes. We urge you to classify VA's delivery of health care as a national security and public safety responsibility, and exempt it from this hiring freeze. To do otherwise is to jeopardize the national security and public safety of our nation.

Source: Letter to President Trump from 53 senators, Jan. 26, 2017

Campaign Promises on Climate Change Treaty

Rejoin Greenhouse Gas Initiative via Clean Power Plan

Today's EPA announcement [to curb carbon emissions] represents a major step forward in our national effort to reduce greenhouse gas emissions and fight climate change. We must be aggressive in our pursuit of reducing our carbon footprint. The [Clean Power Plan] is a common sense proposal that will empower states to do their part and contribute to the national goal of curbing emissions from power plants.

I am also encouraged by the flexibility the administration's plan provides for each state to decide exactly how they will achieve our national goal to reduce emissions from power plants by 30 percent by 2030. In light of today's announcement, New Jersey should consider rejoining the successful Regional Green House Gas Initiative, which would allow us to reduce and offset our carbon emissions by making investments in clean energy. I am confident that New Jersey will achieve the goals presented today and remain a national leader in clean energy production.

Power plants account for roughly one-third of all domestic greenhouse gas emissions in the United States. While there are limits in place for the level of arsenic, mercury, sulfur dioxide, nitrogen oxides, and particle pollution that power plants can emit, there are currently no national limits on carbon pollution levels. By 2030, the Clean Power Plan proposal has set goals that will:

- cut carbon emission from the power sector by 30 percent nationwide below 2005 levels

- cut particle pollution, nitrogen oxides, and sulfur dioxide by more than 25 percent as a co-benefit

- avoid up to 6,600 premature deaths, up to 150,000 asthma attacks in children, and up to 490,000 missed work or school days

- and shrink electricity bills roughly 8 percent by increasing energy efficiency and reducing demand in the electricity system.

Source: Press Release on EPA's Plan to Reduce Carbon Pollution, June 3, 2014

Actions Taken on Climate Change Treaty

Climate change requires American leadership

When I was [in France for the Paris climate talks]over there, I was moved to see virtually all of the globe represented by leaders, NGOs, and major corporations. The planet coming together, focused on this issue of the impacts of climate change. Conversations ranged from focusing on innovative renewable technology, all the way to resiliency for poor populations who are disproportionately affected by climate change.

I had the honor of leading a bilateral conversation with Bangladesh, talking to peer leaders — the United States sitting down at a table with and across the table from ministry and parliamentary members from Bangladesh. By many estimates, Bangladesh is the most vulnerable large country to climate change. Due to climate change [including rising sea levels and ice-pack melting off the Himalayas], right now Bangladesh is losing 1% of its arable land each year, displacing millions of Bangladeshis, literally creating climate refugees.

This is an issue that affects America that we cannot solve without joining with the rest of the globe. American leadership is incredibly needed. I am proud to send a strong message to the rest of the globe that we are here in the United States strongly supporting the ambitious commitments of President Obama, and that we will defend those communities that are facing this crisis. We will be leaders.

Source: Library of Congress transcript of Senate floor speech, Dec. 10, 2015

KEPT PROMISE: *Booker had great expectations for President Obama's climate policy, and followed through as a senator by participating in the latest round of climate talks. How that translates under President Trump is still an open question.*

ANALYSIS: *The 2015 Paris Climate Conference resulted in an international treaty where 194 countries agreed to limit their carbon output. The Paris Agreement continues the method defined under the Kyoto protocol, of setting carbon dioxide reduction via a "cap-and-trade" market for carbon. In 2016, The U.S. and China (the two largest carbon emitters) bilaterally agreed to join the Paris Agreement.*

Campaign Promises on Foreign Diplomacy

No head in the sand; but no global police

Booker and [opponent Mayor Steve] Lonegan in the first debate scoffed at the notion of the U.S. as an international police force. Neither Booker nor Lonegan would qualify as a "hawk," but Booker is more receptive to the deployment of U.S. forces. Asked a Syria-inspired question in the first debate about "America's role in the world," Booker said the U.S. should be willing to combat genocide, while Lonegan countered that the military's role is to "defend our borders and trade routes."

That drew a rebuttal from Booker: "We cannot, like Mr. Lonegan suggests, just stick our heads in the sand and protect our borders. We have to be involved in the international community in a way that works with others to stop terrorism, other problems — famines to genocide — that are going on in the world," Booker said.

Source: WHYY NewsWorks.org on New Jersey Senate race, Oct. 14, 2013

Robust diplomacy and international development

The world is changing. A hyper-connected, interdependent world economy and new technologies have empowered people and organizations. Gone are the days when we worried principally about a single geopolitical foe. We face new, diverse threats, and we must meet them with a smart, principled strategy that recognizes, rather than ignores, how our world is changing.

America is a great nation because, over the course of our history, we have done great things. The tools that made us a world power – a strong economy, a strong military, robust diplomacy with strong allies, international development, and support for democracy – all must have a place in American strategy. Few of the new challenges we face can be solved by our military alone. Instead all of these pieces must work together to address the economic, social, political, and military challenges of our time.

Source: CoryBooker.com Senate campaign website, Nov. 3, 2013

Actions Taken on Foreign Diplomacy

Fund the life-saving work done by diplomats

President Trump's budget would set our country back and make hardworking Americans suffer. If adopted by Congress, it would stifle our nation's economic competitiveness, hurt the most vulnerable among us, and make our country less safe.

By gutting the institutions that protect the rights of workers, Trump's budget would make it more difficult for hardworking people who play by the rules to get a fair shake and make a better life for their family. It would undermine the necessary and life-saving work done by diplomats representing American interests across the globe, making our country less safe and our world less secure. It would slow progress in scientific research, making it more difficult for the United States to lead the charge towards the cure for diseases like cancer.

And in a direct contradiction to his often-repeated promises to invest in American infrastructure, Trump's budget proposes devastating cuts to maintaining our nation's roads, railways, bridges, and ports that will make it more difficult for American companies to compete and succeed. This out-of-touch, callous, and dangerous budget is a reflection of President Trump's skewed political priorities, not what's best for middle class families and our country's economic competitiveness.

Source: Booker press release on Trump Budget, March 16, 2017

KEPT PROMISE: *Booker promised foreign diplomatic engagement and he has followed through in the Senate.*

ANALYSIS: *We characterize Booker as a "multilateralist" who supports international organizations and the American diplomats who populate them. The opposing view, classically called "isolationism" but currently called "American Exceptionalism," supports little engagement abroad other than military alliances and military actions. Above, Booker accuses President Trump of "isolationism": Trump's proposed budget drastically increases the defense budget while cutting just about everything else. For comparison, the Department of Defense's budget is $590 billion, while the Department of State's budget is $30 billion (which includes all diplomatic activities that Booker defends).*

Campaign Promises on Africa Policy

Stable African countries are good for our security

The countries of Africa have some of the fastest growing and most vibrant economies in the world. The story of Africa is one of transformation: local populations, partnered with international organizations and American international development funds, have done enormous good increasing standards of living and improving public health. In few areas has this been truer than the fight against HIV/AIDS, where millions of lives have been saved. Of course, much work remains to be done, particularly when it comes to helping governments drive out corruption and enforce the rule of law.

Expanding the economic pie means creating strong ties with these developing nations. Rather than making these countries dependent on long-term foreign aid, we should focus on increasing trade with them. For example, in countries that don't have legacy landline telephones, as we do in America, there are opportunities to invest in mobile data technology – creating jobs here and there. This "trade, not aid" approach means new markets for American goods, self-sufficient countries that benefit from investment and a world economy that's expanding.

Stronger, more stable African countries are also good for our security. Some parts of Africa, like Mali and Somalia, have had significant problems with extremist groups. Extremists have a much harder time gaining a foothold and recruiting when a countries people are making money, putting food on the table, and being supported by an effective government.

Source: CoryBooker.com Senate campaign website, Nov. 3, 2013

KEPT PROMISE: *Booker expressed an Africa policy during his campaign; and he acted on an Africa policy in the Senate. On this issue, that is a consistent "promise kept."*

ANALYSIS: *Simply HAVING an Africa policy is the remarkable aspect of this issue. Booker's Africa policy is unsurprising since Booker is only the 9th African American to serve in the U.S. Senate, out of 1,298 Senators in U.S. history (by percentage of the population, Booker should have been the 159th African American Senator).*

Actions Taken on Africa Policy

Enforce humanitarian aid access to South Sudan

Since the onset of South Sudan's civil war in 2013, at least 50,000 people have been killed and approximately 3 million have fled their homes. The African Union and the United Nations have documented numerous human rights abuses and warned of potential genocide. The assaults on civilians carried out during the course of the fighting in July 2016 between government and opposition forces shocked the conscience of the world, and served to demonstrate that the August 2015 peace agreement has failed. To date, the government has not held anyone accountable for the violence, nor for attacking a U.S. diplomatic convoy.

UN peacekeepers are protecting over 200,000 people who might otherwise be dead at UN bases in South Sudan. The UN Security Council approved an additional 4,000 peacekeepers in the wake of the July violence. Unfortunately, the government continues to obstruct the deployment of UN troops. Conflict along South Sudan's southern border has resulted in the outflow of nearly 700,000 refugees to Uganda.

In Sudan, it is critical that we ensure that Khartoum lives up to its agreement to adhere to its ceasefires, allow free and unfettered humanitarian access to all parts of Sudan and stop supporting rebel movements in South Sudan. United States leadership is critical to helping bring about a lasting peace in Sudan and South Sudan. Your swift action on this matter will make a difference in millions of lives. We look forward to working with you to address these and other issues.

Source: Letter from 12 senators to President Trump, Feb. 27, 2017

BACKGROUND: *South Sudan is an oil-rich Sub-Saharan nation of about 12 million people, which gained independence in 2011 from Sudan (now known as North Sudan). Independence followed decades of civil war within Sudan; that civil unrest continues in the newly-independent South Sudan. "Khartoum" above refers to the capital of North Sudan (also of pre-secession Sudan); Juba is the capital city of South Sudan. North Sudan is majority Muslim; South Sudan is majority Christian and animist (this pattern is common in countries that span the Sahara to the south). The religious differences played a factor in the split between the two nations.*

Campaign Promises on China Policy

China cheats via currency manipulation & IP theft

America's relationship with China will, in many ways, define the next century of American security. As China expands its economy, grows its military, and competes on the world stage, it is essential for them to play by the rules. Thankfully, China needs us – our economy remains the most powerful in the world – and there are countless areas where our countries cooperate to advance shared priorities.

American workers can compete and win on a level playing field, which is why China's cheating – through artificially depressing its currency and other unfair trade practices – is so damaging. While currency appreciation has occurred, keeping it artificially low hurts our economic competitiveness and undermines the trust that is essential to a strong relationship. That doesn't mean we should start a trade war – that would hurt our economy just as much as it would hurt China's. Instead, our goal should be a level playing field that treats everyone fairly, and that includes cracking down on unfair practices, such as unreasonable market barriers and Intellectual Property theft, that often break China's commitments to us and the rest of the world.

Source: CoryBooker.com Senate campaign website, Nov. 3, 2013

BACKGROUND: *China, the world's largest Communist country, will soon become the world's largest economy (estimated to pass the U.S. in 2024). Since 2010, China's economy has grown at an annual rate of 6% or 7%, despite the lingering Great Recession (which only slowed China's growth slightly) – compare that to U.S. and European growth rates of 1% or 2% annually. U.S. trade with China totaled $579 billion in 2016, but with a $347 billion trade deficit. The U.S. has issues with China on currency manipulation, export dumping, and labor conditions within China. Those trade-related issues will dominate U.S.-China relations in the 2018 campaign and afterwards.*

Actions Taken on China Policy

Resolve disputes so US can export solar panels to China

Seven senators [including Booker] this week called on Vice President Joe Biden to help settle a trade dispute between the U.S. and China over solar equipment and goods. Excerpts from their letter:

The dispute with China over solar goods continues to escalate. China continues to demonstrate an unwillingness to settle the dispute until our domestic solar industry presents unified proposals that remove existing trade restrictions. Therefore, we ask you to bring folks together to develop a negotiated settlement that will lead to growth in all aspects of the solar industry.

Earlier this year, the Department of Commerce commenced another round of anti-dumping investigations into Chinese solar panels, which will likely lead to additional tariffs and further retaliation from the Chinese. Continuing to let this dispute play out one case at a time will limit job growth and it may even lead to job loss.

The solar industry is experiencing remarkable growth, employing 140,000 workers last year, a 20% increase from the previous year. We want to see all areas of the industry continue to create high-paying jobs for Americans.

Source: Letter to Vice President Biden from 7 senators, April 9, 2014

BROKEN PROMISE: *Booker talked tough on China during the campaign, but caved in when it came to actually negotiating a deal. We label this an "**evolution**" where Booker accepted that dealing with China gave more leverage than pressuring China from a stand-off position.*

ANALYSIS: *Comparing the two contrasting statements, Booker is in effect saying "China cheats – but let's deal with them anyway." Comparing the excerpt above with Booker's anti-dumping stance on p. 128, Booker is in effect saying "Investigate China for dumping – just not on solar panels." Booker's campaign statements support "fair trade" — rewriting the rules – whereas his actions support "free trade" – making SOME sort of deal despite whatever problems come up.*

Campaign Promises on Fair Trade

Fight foreign predatory trade practices on car tires

We are writing in strong support of the Department's [of Commerce] decision to initiate antidumping and countervailing duty investigations of passenger vehicle and light truck tires from China.

China has targeted the passenger vehicle and light truck tire sector for development and there are several hundred tire manufacturing facilities now operating in that country. In 2009, the United Steelworkers (USW) sought relief from a flood of similar tires from China that were injuring our producers and their workers.

Unfortunately, shortly after relief expired in 2012, imports of these tires from China once again skyrocketed: imports from China have roughly doubled. In June 2014, the USW alleged dumping and subsidies, identifying dumping margins as high as 87% and provided sufficient information for the Department to initiate an investigation on 39 separate subsidies available to tire producers in China. Our laws need to be fairly and faithfully enforced to ensure that workers can be confident that, when they work hard and play by the rules, their government will stand by their side to fight foreign predatory trade practices.

America's laws against unfair trade are a critical underpinning of our economic policies and economic prosperity. Given the chance, American workers can out-compete anyone. But, in the face of China's continual targeting of our manufacturing base, we need to make sure that we act quickly and enforce our laws. That is what we are asking and urge you and your Department to carefully analyze the facts and act to restore fair conditions for trade.

Source: Letter from 31 senators to Sec'y of Commerce, Sept. 16, 2014

KEPT PROMISE: *Booker's campaign promised to fight unfair trade, and he has done so – when it comes to individual products. He makes exceptions for China (pp. 126-7) and for trade promotion (pp. 130-1), indicating that he is not a hard-core ideological "fair trader," but instead focused on assisting particular industries (such as those with heavy employment in New Jersey).*

Actions Taken on Fair Trade

Declare Turkish rebar subject to anti-dumping duties

We write to you regarding countervailing duty and antidumping investigations being conducted by the U.S. Department of Commerce on imports of steel reinforcing bar (rebar) from Turkey and Mexico. American businesses and workers expect that the Department will find dumping and subsidization where it is occurring, and will prosecute unfair trade practices to the full extent of the law.

Rebar is one of the largest volume steel products produced in the U.S., employing more than 10,000 workers in over 30 states. With nearly 7 million tons of domestic production, a healthy rebar industry is critical to a strong economy. However, it is our understanding that imports from Turkey and Mexico are surging into the U.S., nearly doubling from 2011 to 2013. The widespread impact these unfairly-traded rebar imports are having on industry and communities across the country is extremely troubling and must be addressed.

The International Trade Commission recently found that Mexican and Turkish rebar producers are consistently underselling U.S. producers, resulting in substantial lost sales and depressed prices. Subsequently, the Department of Commerce made a preliminary finding that the Government of Turkey bestows energy subsidies to its rebar industry, but that such subsidies are only *de minimis* in value. This seems surprising given the inherently energy-intensive nature of steel production. It is essential that we do everything to prevent unfairly-traded imports from negatively impacting good-paying American jobs. We urge you to take the necessary actions to strictly and fully enforce our trade laws.

Source: Letter from 31 senators to the Secretary of Commerce, April 9, 2014

ANALYSIS: *Let's say Booker is right, and China, Turkey, and Mexico "dump" products in the U.S. Who does that hurt? Sure, the particular corporations who compete with them. But for consumers, this "dumping" means lower prices – in this case, cheaper tires and homes. In general, free trade means some companies and workers are hurt but consumers always benefit – which means Booker's "fair trade" only protects corporations!*

Campaign Promises on Trade Promotion

No fast-track for Trans-Pacific Partnership

U.S. Sen. Cory Booker broke with President Obama and voted against giving him new authority to negotiate trade legislation. Booker voted against giving Obama the ability to negotiate the Trans-Pacific Partnership and bring it back to Congress for an up-or-down vote without amendments, a process known as fast-track or trade promotion authority. The bill passed Friday night, 62-37, with just 14 Democrats supporting it.

Booker, given the choice of supporting the president or his progressive allies, joined most Senate Democrats in voting no. "Our trade policy must balance the need to increase exports and expand commerce with provisions that empower American workers," Booker said in a statement after the vote. "This trade promotion authority legislation did not provide enough assurance that a deal reached under its terms would achieve that balance."

The Trans-Pacific Partnership would lower trade barriers among the U.S. and 12 nations, including Canada, Mexico, Japan, New Zealand and Vietnam. The Obama administration has touted it as a way to grow the U.S. economy and create jobs

Source: Newark Star Ledger, "Booker opposes Obama's trade bill,"
May 23, 2015

BROKEN PROMISE: *Booker opposes multilateral trade deals, but supports export promotion – that's a **legalism in** that he is technically FOR free trade on the export side, but AGAINST free trade on the import side.*

ANALYSIS: *Booker's pro-export anti-import policy actually has a name – "neomercantilism" – which differentiates Booker from what seems to be "protectionism" on the previous pages. Protectionists believe in limiting all trade (in both directions); mercantilists believe in limiting imports but favoring exports. That's in line with Booker's pro-corporate outlook: mercantilism helps American corporations at the expense of foreign corporations (and at the expense of consumers). Both protectionists and mercantilists call themselves "fair traders" but they differ in this key aspect.*

Actions Taken on Trade Promotion

$25B more loans from Export-Import Bank

Booker voted to support S.824: This bill raises the cap on outstanding loans, guarantees, and insurance of the Export-Import Bank of the United States for FY2015-FY2022 and afterwards. The Bank shall:

- Provide technical assistance to small businesses on how to apply for financial assistance from the Bank;

- Establish programs under which private financial institutions may share risk in the loans, guarantees, and other Bank products in exchange for receiving fees received from program participants.

- The Bank may enter into up to $25 billion worth of contracts of reinsurance, co-finance, or other risk-sharing arrangements on its portfolio or individual transactions with insurance companies, financial institutions, or export credit agencies.

Opponents reasons for voting NAY: (Washington Examiner, 12/2/12): The Export-Import Bank is a taxpayer-backed agency that finances U.S. exports, primarily though loan guarantees. You'd think the bank would spread the money around to nurture up-and-coming businesses. You'd be wrong, very wrong. In fact, 83% of its taxpayer-backed loan guarantees in 2012 went to just one exporter: Boeing. Welcome to the "New Economic Patriotism," where the big get bigger and taxpayers bear the risk. Ex-Im is at the heart of Obama's National Export Initiative and is a pillar of the economic patriotism that Obama pledged in a second term. When government hands out more money, the guys with the best lobbyists and the closest ties to power will disproportionately get their hands on that money.

Source: Promoting U.S. Jobs Through Exports Act, H.R.1031 & S.824: Booker voted NAY on replacement bill S.819 on Oct. 19, 2015

BACKGROUND: *The Ex-Im Bank is a federal agency which provides financing for American companies exporting goods and services overseas. Their purpose to provide credit for companies that can't get credit from normal banks because of political risk or economic risk. Despite their name, the Ex-Im Bank does not provide any assistance for imports – only for exports. Critics call the Ex-Im Bank "corporate welfare."*

Campaign Promises on Immigration Reform

Blocking the DREAM Act is crazy;
it's how we built America

[Commenting on the Republicans' blocking passage of the DREAM Act], "These are people who want to serve in the military and get educated. Forget the politics. It's the pragmatism of it. We are a nation that has built our country on immigrants from Einstein to some of our greatest scientists have been people coming in. And to tell people who have been through high school and high school presidents going to college [and who have served on the front lines] this is crazy."

Source: Interview with NBC News' Andrea Mitchell, Dec. 19, 2010

BACKGROUND: *President Obama issued Executive Orders deferring deportation of five million illegal immigrants who came to America as minors (known as DREAMers, for the DREAM Act). Opponents claim Obama unconstitutionally bypassed Congress. Supporters claim that Congress failed to pass comprehensive reforms for years, so Obama had to act unilaterally.*

The two main Executive Orders are known as DACA and DAPA: Deferred Action for Childhood Arrivals, which ensured that DREAMers would not get deported; and Deferred Action for Parents of Americans, which ensured that their parents would not be deported, either. DACA was signed in 2012; DAPA was signed in 2015, along with an expansion of DACA.

KEPT PROMISE: *Booker supported the DREAM Act during his campaign; he followed up with support of Obama's Executive Actions during his Senate tenure, as well as calls for comprehensive legislation. This implies that Booker opposes President Trump's reversal of DACA and DAPA; no comprehensive reform legislation is likely in the 2017-2018 Congress.*

Actions Taken on Immigration Reform

Supports Executive Action;
prefers comprehensive strategy

I am encouraged by President Obama's remarks tonight on immigration reform. This is an important first step and more needs to be done. At a time of great crisis in our country, when families are being separated, our nation is losing revenue, and we have an immigration policy that by just about everyone's account is failing to accomplish our common goals, we must implement a comprehensive strategy that secures our border and strengthens our economy.

The president's plan will greatly help law enforcement focus on felons and threats to our country, and pull individuals out of the shadows, not to grant them amnesty, but allow them to pay taxes and start on a path towards lawful immigration. Congress must act to fix our broken immigration system and implement a long-term solution — nothing less than America's economic success, national security, and fundamental values are at stake. Senator Menendez and a bipartisan coalition in the Senate have already passed a comprehensive immigration bill, and now it's time for House Republicans to act.

Source: Booker press release on Immigration Executive Action,
Nov. 21, 2014

ANALYSIS: *Comprehensive reform (which Booker advocates above) is a politicized buzzword that means "provide amnesty and citizenship benefits for illegal immigrants already here, while securing the border and prosecuting illegal employers against new illegal immigration." Opponents of comprehensive reform would prefer a piecemeal approach: their buzzword is "secure the border first," before dealing with any benefits or any other issues.*

Comprehensive reform did not pass Congress under President Obama; hence leaving the issue to Obama's Executive Orders. President Trump overturned Obama's Executive Orders on immigration, and instituted new immigration restrictions as well. Booker's support of Obama's Executive Action means he supports DACA and DAPA.

Campaign Promises on Sanctuary Cities

Against involving city police in immigration matters

To the revelation that a suspect in the Newark shootings, Jose Lachira Carranza, is an illegal immigrant from Peru who could have been detained by federal immigration authorities after he was arrested three times on criminal charges, a national chorus reacted with horror to the Aug. 4 killings at a playground here. The mayor of Newark, Cory A. Booker, has tried to keep the public discussion focused on his main goal: reducing the crime rate. Mr. Booker said he was frustrated that Mr. Carranza had been responding to the debate surrounding the suspect's illegal status, and has come out firmly against involving city police in immigration matters. He said such a role would hurt relationships with what he called "the most marginalized and vulnerable people within our community."

"My police department does not play an I.N.S. function," Mr. Booker said. "We are not to be running around doing interrogations about whether someone is documented or not."

Source: Kareem Fahim in New York Times, "Newark Triple Murder",
Aug 19, 2007

BACKGROUND: The term "sanctuary city" is a political term with ambiguous legal meaning (and the post-Trump political term is shifting to "welcoming city" or "trust city"). The only federal law on the topic disallows city ordinances and state laws that would prohibit sharing information on immigrants possessed by the city or state. In other words, there is no obligation to GATHER information on immigration status, but only a requirement to share what has been gathered. President Trump asserts that sanctuary cities violate federal law, but that is only true if they explicitly ban cooperation with federal authorities. Cities are free to declare that their local police should not ask about immigration status, in order to encourage cooperation by undocumented immigrants in police investigations. Most sanctuary city laws focus on that aspect of local policing, including Mayor Booker's policy in Newark above.

Actions Taken on Sanctuary Cities

Legal help, at government expense, for aliens being deported

Booker co-sponsored S.2540/H.R.4646: authorizing the Department of Justice (DOJ) to appoint or provide counsel at government expense to aliens in removal proceedings.

- The Department of Homeland Security (DHS) shall provide an alien in removal proceedings with all relevant documents in its possession, unless the alien has knowingly waived the right to such documents.

- DOJ may appoint or provide counsel to aliens in any INA proceeding.

- DHS shall ensure that aliens have access to counsel inside all immigration detention and border facilities.

- DOJ shall appoint counsel, at government expense if necessary, for an unaccompanied alien child or a particularly vulnerable individual.

- DHS shall establish a pilot program to increase the court appearance rates of unaccompanied alien children and particularly vulnerable individuals by contracting with nongovernmental, community-based organizations to provide such aliens with case management services.

Source: Fair Day in Court for Kids Act on Feb. 11, 2016

KEPT PROMISE: *Mayor Booker took action to assist undocumented immigrants locally in Newark; Senator Booker took action to assist undocumented immigrants nationwide.*

ANALYSIS: *The only federal legislative proposals on sanctuary cities per se has been in opposition; Booker has not co-sponsored any, and none have yet come to a vote.*

Campaign Promises on Syrian Refugees

Welcome Syrian refugees and fight any bans

Sen. Cory Booker, rejecting arguments from Gov. Chris Christie and other Republicans, said Syrian refugees should be welcomed into the country. "It belies who we are as a nation to turn them away," Booker said. "It's an insult to our history. It's unacceptable to me."

Christie and other Republican governors have said they won't accept any of at least 10,000 Syrian refugees that President Obama wants to allow to emigrate to the U.S. "I will fight anyone who wants to shut down this nation's open arms," Booker said. Booker said that any refugee wanting to settle in the U.S. undergoes a background check of 18 months to two years. "There's a thorough vetting process," he said.

House Republicans have introduced two bills to keep the Syrian refugees out of the U.S. One would prevent any refugees from coming to the U.S., and another would require that priority for Iraqis and Syrians go to "members of a persecuted religious minority." Booker was among the U.S. senators last month who supported emergency funding to help Syrian refugees. Booker was among the lawmakers in October who urged Obama to make it easier for refugees to reunite with relatives already in the U.S.

Source: Newark Star-Ledger, "Refugee Ban Belies Who We Are," Nov. 17, 2015

BACKGROUND: *The Syrian refugee crisis resulted from the Syrian civil war, which has been raging since 2011. ISIS occupies large areas of Syria as well as areas in Iraq. Million of refugees have fled the war; destabilizing neighboring Turkey, Lebanon, and Jordan, with over a million refugees each, and another million refugees ending up in Europe.*

KEPT PROMISE: *Booker promised to welcome refugees from the Syrian civil war, and he has remained involved in that issue in the Senate.*

ANALYSIS: *This issue straddles immigration policy (see pp. 132-3) and war policy (see pp. 110-1). It's very easy to become self-contradictory in those paired policies – such as calling for military force in Syria without accepting the refugees that action causes – but so far Booker has successfully straddled that line.*

Actions Taken on Syrian Refugees

No right to ban immigrants based on [Muslim] religion

Booker co-sponsored the Freedom of Religion Act; **Congressional Summary:** An alien may not be denied admission to the US because of the alien's religion or lack of religious beliefs.

Argument Opposed: [Countable.us]: The U.S. should reserve the right to ban immigrants based on religion. The government may need to enact such a ban in response to a future acts of terror, which could save American lives.

Argument In Favor: [Cato Institute, Dec. 8, 2016]: Donald Trump proposed prohibiting all Muslim immigration. However, under current law, it is illegal to discriminate against immigrants based on their national origin. Congress has debated creating an immigration system free from discrimination by country of birth or country of residence. President-elect Trump, however, now proposes to discriminate against certain foreign nationals on the basis of the same protected grounds.

Source: S.54 & H.R.5207, Freedom of Religion Act, Jan. 5, 2017

Hold Assad accountable for slaughter of civilians

A February 7 Amnesty International report asserts that up to 13,000 people have been methodically executed at the Saydnaya Prison as part of a calculated campaign of extrajudicial execution authorized at the highest levels of the Syrian government. This report comes after the 2014 "Caesar Report," which extensively documented the systematic killing of more than 11,000 detainees.

Taken together with credible, clear, and convincing previous reports of Assad's actions — including the confirmed use of chemical weapons — sufficient documentation exists to charge Bashar al-Assad with war crimes and crimes against humanity.

Russia, [despite its support of the Assad regime], must join the international community in seeking to hold Assad accountable, stop enabling the slaughter of the Syrian people, and undertake efforts to remove Iran-affiliated fighters from Syria.

Source: Letter from 14 senators to the Secretary of State, Feb. 22, 2017

Chapter Five: Cory Booker
Promises Kept vs. Promises Broken
on VoteMatch

VoteMatch is our 20-question quiz which summarizes the candidate's views on the controversial issues of the day. The 20 questions appear on the left, with our summary answers for Booker's campaign promises compared to his actions taken, along with the reasons for the shift between them, when there is one. In summary terms of political philosophy, Cory Booker campaigned as a moderate liberal, but governs as a libertarian-leaning progressive:

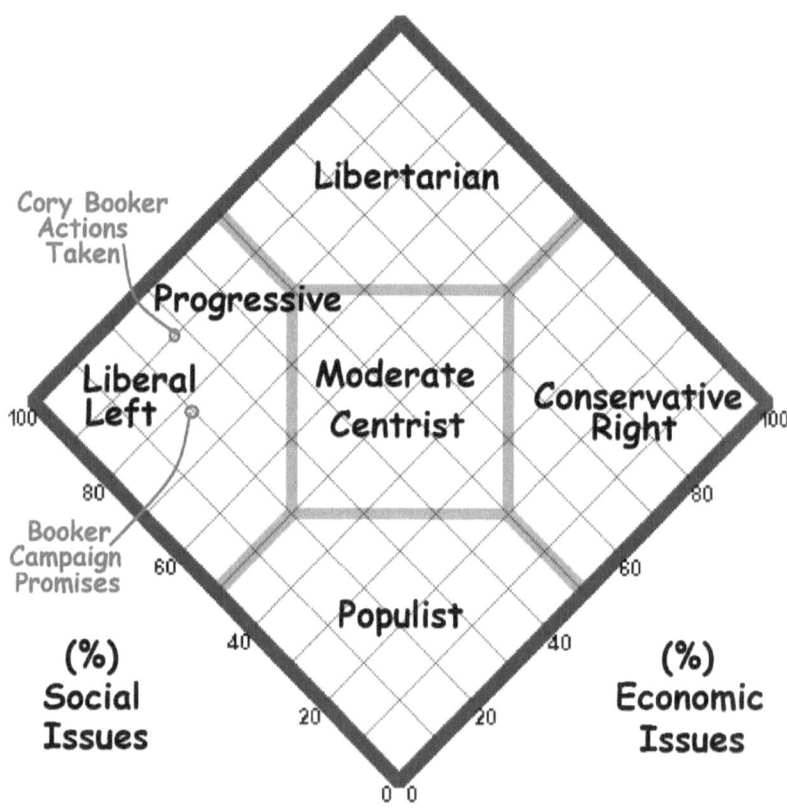

The tables on the following pages illustrate how our political philosophy ranking came about. Our methodology is entirely transparent: we provide enough information here that you can reproduce our conclusions yourself. The steps to produce our VoteMatch chart are:

- Each VoteMatch question of the 20 questions summarizes a series of statements that determine whether Booker supports or opposes that VoteMatch question.

- The average of the series of statements makes up the VoteMatch response, ranging from *strongly oppose* to *strongly favor*. We round *up* to make the overall answer: if there's a hint of strong support, the overall score is *strongly favor* instead of *favor*.

- Not all of the series of statements appear in this book, because we only include statements that have distinguishable campaign promises vs. actions taken. And statements in this book don't necessarily fit into one VoteMatch question. You can see all of the statements that make up Booker's **Campaign Promise** VoteMatch scores, with links to the original context, on our website at http://www.OnTheIssues.org/Senate/Cory_Booker.htm

- We sum up a political philosophy by counting each VoteMatch question based on **Campaign Promises**, on a social scale or an economic scale (ten questions on each scale). This two-dimensional analysis accounts for the usual left-right spectrum as well as a distinction among libertarians, populists, and moderates – a full explanation of the theory and methodology appears below.

- You might disagree with how we score an individual statement, or you might disagree with which VoteMatch category we place it in – but you can see our choices, and those are the only political judgments we make – averaging the scores and summing up into a political philosophy is a mechanical process after those initial judgments are made (and we describe those mechanics below).

- For topics where Booker's actions taken differ from his campaign promises, we assign each broken promise to one VoteMatch category, and each one affects the VoteMatch result by one "tick": moving from *strongly favor* to just *favor*, for example, or from *oppose* to *mixed opinion*.

- Using the same mechanical process as for Booker's campaign promises, we sum up his scores for **Actions Taken** and conclude with a political philosophy differentiating Booker's promises from his governance.

VoteMatch Social Issues

Social Part 1	Campaign Promises	Actions Taken
*Abortion is a woman's unrestricted right	favors	strongly favors due to broken promise on restrictions (p.80)
Comfortable with same-sex marriage	strongly favors	strongly favors
Make voter registration easier	strongly favors	strongly favors
Pathway to citizenship for illegal aliens	strongly favors	strongly favors
Avoid foreign entanglements	strongly favors	strongly favors

Social Part 2	Campaign Promises	Actions Taken
*Stricter punishment reduces crime	supports	opposes due to broken promises on crime theory (p.16) and first responders (p.20)
*Support the War on Drugs	strongly opposes	opposes due to broken promise on opioid crisis (p.28)
*Keep God in the public sphere	mixed opinion	opposes due to broken promise on religious freedom (p.90)
EPA overreach hurts America	strongly opposes	strongly opposes
*Expand the military	supports	opposes due to broken promise on veterans policy (p.114) and defense spending (p.116)

VoteMatch Economic Issues

Economic Part 1	Campaign Promises	Actions Taken
*Privatize Social Security	opposes	strongly opposes due to broken promise on retirement age (p.106)
*Absolute right to gun ownership	strongly opposes	opposes due to broken promise on mass shootings (p.14)
*Vouchers for school choice	mixed opinion	strongly favors due to broken promise on union policy (p.68), Race to the Top (p. 98), and vouchers (p. 102)
*Support & expand free trade	strongly opposes	mixed opinion due to broken promise on trade promotion (p.130) and China policy (p.126)
Support American Exceptionalism	opposes	opposes

Economic Part 2	Campaign Promises	Actions Taken
*Higher taxes on the wealthy	mixed opinion	favors due to broken promise on tax reform (p.62)
Stimulus better than market-led recovery	favors	favors
*Prioritize green energy	favors	strongly favors due to broken promise on carbon tax (p.56)
Legally require hiring women & minorities	strongly favors	strongly favors
*Expand ObamaCare	strongly favors	favors due to broken promise on single payer (p.66)

In our online quiz, you fill in your answers for these 20 questions, and we match you against all the candidates (including Cory Booker and a dozen other contenders and withdrawn contenders from both parties). You can see our online version at:

http://quiz.ontheissues.org/

Below, we've created an on-paper version of the online quiz, where, with a pencil and just a little bit of math, you can get the same result as the online quiz. We also further explain how to convert your VoteMatch answers into a political philosophy, and some additional details about how our two-dimensional political analysis works.

Your Political Philosophy

We hope that this book encourages you, as voters, to make your decisions based on the issues. We recognize the reality of American politics: voters make their decisions based primarily on whether they like the candidates. Accordingly, our goal is to get voters to compare their issue preferences in comparison to candidate issue stances when considering which candidates to like.

We intentionally omitted from this book any biographical background on Senator Booker. Details of politicians' birthplaces and religious affiliations — and minutiae of every other personal detail — are readily available in the mainstream media. Their issue stances are more challenging for voters to find.

Why does the mainstream media fail at this important function? Because they are "news" organizations which are poorly suited to covering political campaigns. "News" implies reporting on what is "new": Booker's stance on marijuana legalization has not changed since 2009 (see pp. 24-5), and his stance on LGBT issues has not changed since 1992 (see p. 88), so there's nothing in the news about those issues. But if you are impassioned about the Drug War, or if you vote based on gay rights, then you cannot rely on the news media for those non-newsworthy issues. And that's where we come in.

Furthermore, the mainstream media interpret candidates using a one-dimensional "right-left" analysis. That simplistic analysis comes to nonsensical conclusions like calling Hillary Clinton "extreme left-wing" even though she supported the Iraq War; supports free trade; and supports faith-based initiatives.

We find our two-dimensional analysis to be more accurate in differentiating candidates than that traditional one-dimensional analysis. We don't claim that our method is perfect — just superior to the simplistic mainstream media. VoteMatch uses a Social Issues dimension plus an Economic Issues dimension; we interpret candidates based on whether they believe in government involvement in either or both of those dimensions. Using the two-dimensional analysis differentiates five classes of political beliefs:

1. **Libertarian:** focusing on non-governmental solutions and private decision-making in both the social and economic dimensions.
   - No government involvement in personal social issues
   - No government involvement in economic issues

2. **Conservative or rightist view:** focusing on fiscal frugality plus moral integrity; with government intervention acceptable in social matters.
   - Government involvement in social issues
   - No government involvement in economic issues

3. **Liberal or leftist view:** focusing on helping needy members of society, and using government to achieve societal good in economic matters
   - No government involvement in personal social issues
   - Government involvement in economic issues
   - "Progressives" fall between liberals and libertarians

4. **Populist:** typically focusing on local solutions instead of federal action, on decentralizing power, and on religion as the basis for societal good.
   - Government involvement in social issues
   - Government involvement in economic issues

5. **Centrist / Moderate:** typically focusing on reforming or amending existing institutions rather than replacing them.
   - Some government involvement in social issues
   - Some government involvement in economic issues

Our VoteMatch quiz summarizes each candidate's issue stances into a summary "political philosophy," based on scoring 20 questions on both a social scale and a political scale. For Cory Booker:

Based on Campaign Promises...   Cory Booker is a moderate liberal

Based on Actions Taken...   Cory Booker is a libertarian-leaning progressive

So how did we get those political philosophy descriptions for him, and how can you make a political philosophy description for yourself? Answer the 20 questions below for yourself — using the scale: favor / strongly favor / oppose / strongly oppose / mixed opinion—then follow the instructions....

VoteMatch Social Issues: Part 1

These "social issues" are those which liberals and libertarians favor, while conservatives and populists oppose them. The questions are worded such that "favor" implies less government intervention, and "oppose" implies more government intervention. Our VoteMatch theory: Liberals and libertarians favor less government intervention on social issues; while conservatives and populists favor more government intervention on social issues.

	Campaign Promises	Actions Taken	You
*Abortion is a woman's unrestricted right	favors (+2½)	strongly favors (+5)	
Comfortable with same-sex marriage	strongly favors (+5)	strongly favors (+5)	
Make voter registration easier	strongly favors (+5)	strongly favors (+5)	
Pathway to citizenship for illegal aliens	strongly favors (+5)	strongly favors (+5)	
Avoid foreign entanglements	strongly favors (+5)	strongly favors (+5)	

VoteMatch Social Issues: Part 2

These "social issues" are those which liberals and libertarians oppose, while conservatives and populists favor. The questions are worded such that "oppose" implies less government intervention, and "favor" implies more government intervention.

	Campaign Promises	Actions Taken	You
*Stricter punishment reduces crime	supports (-2½)	opposes (+2½)	
*Support the War on Drugs	strongly opposes (+5)	opposes (+2½)	
*Keep God in the public sphere	mixed opinion (+0)	opposes (+2½)	
EPA overreach hurts America	strongly opposes (+5)	strongly opposes (+5)	
*Expand the military	supports (-2½)	opposes (+2½)	

VoteMatch Social Score

At this point, you've completed all of the social issue questions, and you're ready to get your VoteMatch social score. In Social Part 1, score each answer as follows: +5 for strongly favor; +2½ for favor; +0 for mixed opinion; -2½ for oppose; -5 for strongly oppose. In Social Part 2, switch the scores for favor vs. oppose (-5 for strongly favor through +5 for strongly oppose). Add them up and then add 50, to "normalize" the scale to 0 through 100. We've done all that for Cory Booker below:

	Campaign Promises	Actions Taken	You
Raw social score (add up all scores)	27½	40	
Normalized social score (add 50 to raw score)	77½	90	

VoteMatch Economic Issues: Part 1

These "economic issues" are those which liberals and populists oppose, while conservatives and libertarians favor. The questions are worded such that "favor" implies less government intervention, and "oppose" implies more government intervention. Note that on economic topics, liberals match populists, while in social topics, they are opposite.

	Campaign Promises	Actions Taken	You
*Privatize Social Security	opposes (-2½)	strongly opposes (-5)	
*Absolute right to gun ownership	strongly opposes (-5)	opposes (-2½)	
*Vouchers for school choice	mixed opinion (+0)	strongly favors (+5)	
*Support & expand free trade	strongly opposes (-5)	mixed opinion (+0)	
Support American Exceptionalism	opposes (-2½)	opposes (-2½)	

A word about methodology: the reason the questions are split into two groups for each scale is to avoid "yes bias." People like answering "yes" to questions more than they like answering "no." If a quiz has questions which are all answered "yes," that is called a "push poll," because it "pushes" you towards its desired result. We balance our VoteMatch quiz so that it does not "push" you to any particular ideology.

Nonetheless, looking at current politicians, there are very few populists: Donald Trump is as close as anyone comes. True populists are a thing of the past: you can see from the quiz questions that they would call for government economic intervention as well as government social intervention – that would include the no-longer active movement called "the religious left." Perhaps we'll see a resurgence of the religious left – or the growth of the progressive movement – in either case, VoteMatch will differentiate them, while a single-dimensional left-right analysis will not!

VoteMatch Economic Issues: Part 2

	Campaign Promises	Actions Taken	You
*Higher taxes on the wealthy	mixed opinion (+0)	favors (-2½)	
Stimulus better than market-led recovery	Favors (-2½)	favors (-2½)	
*Prioritize green energy	Favors (-2½)	strongly favors (-5)	
Legally require hiring women & minorities	strongly favors (-5)	strongly favors (-5)	
*Expand ObamaCare	strongly favors (-5)	favors (-2½)	

VoteMatch Economic Score

At this point, you've completed all of the economic issue questions, and you're ready to get your VoteMatch economic score, and then combine it with your social score. In Economic Part 1, score each answer: -5 for strongly favor; -2½ for favor; +0 for mixed opinion; +2½ for oppose; +5 for strongly oppose. In Economic Part 2, switch the scores for favor vs. oppose (+5 for strongly favor through -5 for strongly oppose). Add them up and then add 50, to "normalize" the scale to 0 through 100 (skip the ½'s in your total). We've done all that for the candidates below:

	Campaign Promises	Actions Taken	You
Raw economic score (add up all scores)	-30	-22½	
Normalized economic score (add 50 to raw score)	20	27½	

VoteMatch Chart

Now you're ready to plot your two scores on the VoteMatch chart, and identify your political philosophy. Start at the bottom of the diamond (the point labeled 0/0). Slide up the Social Issues scale until you match your normalized social score; mark that point on the axis. Then start at that point on the axis, and slide along the diagonal grid until the Economic Issues scale matches your normalized economic score: that is your overall political philosophy. If your economic score is higher than your social score, it's easier to start with the economic score first, then slide along the diagonal lines for the social score. We've done it for Cory Booker below:

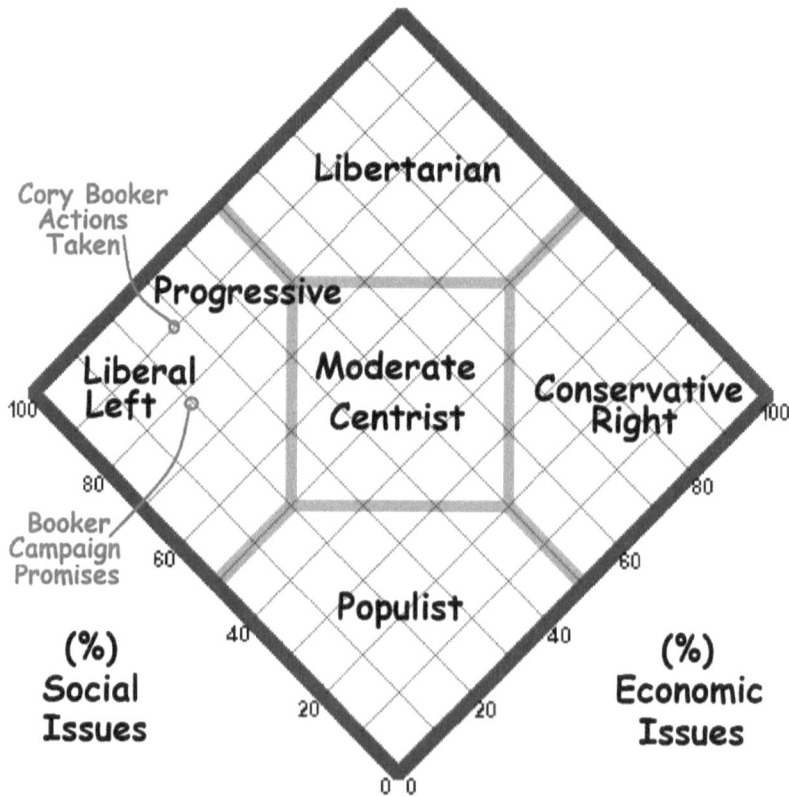

Based on Campaign Promises...   Cory Booker is a moderate liberal

Based on Actions Taken...   Cory Booker is a
libertarian-leaning progressive

You can come up with a description of your political philosophy depending on which quadrant your final score falls in. We describe extremes in any direction as "hard core" (so a social score of 90 and an economic score of 10 is a "hard core liberal") and if you're towards the middle, describe yourself as a "moderate" (so a social score of 30 and an economic score of 70 is a "moderate conservative"). If you're halfway between the quadrants, mix the terms (so a social score of 90 and an economic score of 50 is a "libertarian-leaning liberal"). Our online quiz (see www.ontheissues.org/quiz) uses all those terms and adds a few more – use this as a guide – with a grain of salt!

Other Books

- Trump and Pence vs. Clinton and Kaine On the Issues

- Donald Trump (R) vs. Hillary Clinton (D) vs. Jill Stein (G) vs. Gary Johnson (L) On the Issues

- Hillary Clinton vs. Bernie Sanders On the Issues

Acknowledgments

This book would not have been possible without the tireless efforts of the entire OnTheIssues team: Will Hayes, Joshua Hoerr (our App designer), Marissa Hoerr (our Facebook consultant), Daniel M. Kimmel, Ram Lau, Rachael Lawrence, Jamie Leighton, Naomi Lichtenberg, Laura Nagel (our cover artist), Ogden Porter, Will Rico, Dan Teittinen, and Irma Teittinen.

About the Editor

Jesse Gordon has been the editor-in-chief of OnTheIssues.org since its formation in 1999. His passion revolves around providing issue-based coverage on political races, to combat the mainstream media's growing lack of such coverage.

Mr. Gordon holds a Master's degree in Public Policy from Harvard University's Kennedy School of Government. He and the website OnTheIssues.org are based in Cambridge, Massachusetts.

Mr. Gordon's politics are, on the VoteMatch chart, a libertarian-leaning progressive (upper left quadrant). He is a registered Independent, but has voted for Democrats, Republicans, Greens, and Libertarians. He was the founder of both the Progressive Democrats of Cambridge, and the Harvard University Libertarian Caucus. His most important political values are open government, as reflected in the open issues concept underlying the OnTheIssues website.

Mr. Gordon replies to email personally, at jesse@ontheissues.org — whether to suggest improvements to the website or to order one of the other books above.